Retail Revolution: Navigating the Future of Retail

Modern day living is a multifaceted compendium of evolving technology and social media

Tony Bruno

Table Of Contents

Chapter 1: The Landscape of Retail Franchising — 2

Chapter 2: Food and Beverage Franchising — 7

Chapter 3: Health and Fitness Franchising — 13

Chapter 4: Retail Franchising Essentials — 19

Chapter 5: Service-Based Franchising — 25

Chapter 6: Home-Based Franchising — 31

Chapter 7: Technology and E-commerce Franchising — 37

Chapter 8: Education and Tutoring Franchising — 43

Chapter 9: Pet Care Franchising — 49

Chapter 10: Real Estate Franchising — 54

Chapter 11: Travel and Hospitality Franchising — 59

Chapter 12: Financing Your Franchise — 64

Chapter 13: Marketing Strategies for Franchise Success — 70

Chapter 14: Scaling and Expanding Your Franchise — 76

Chapter 15: Future Trends in Retail Franchising — 81

01

Chapter 1: The Landscape of Retail Franchising

Understanding Franchising Models

Franchising models represent a diverse array of business structures that provide unique opportunities for entrepreneurs and investors. At its core, franchising allows individuals to operate a business under an established brand while leveraging the operational support and marketing expertise of the franchisor. This symbiotic relationship benefits both parties, as franchisees gain access to a proven business model, and franchisors expand their brand presence with relatively low capital investment. Understanding the various franchising models is crucial for those looking to navigate the complexities of the retail landscape.

One prevalent model is the single-unit franchise, where an individual invests in a single location of a franchise brand. This model is ideal for entrepreneurs looking to manage a business closely and maintain a hands-on approach. It allows for a focused operational strategy and the opportunity to build strong relationships with customers and staff. In contrast, the multi-unit franchise model enables franchisees to operate several locations simultaneously, presenting greater revenue potential and economies of scale. This model is particularly appealing to seasoned entrepreneurs seeking to expand their footprint in the market.

Another significant model is the area development franchise, which grants franchisees the rights to open multiple units within a specific geographic area. This approach combines the advantages of multi-unit franchising with a regional focus, allowing franchisees to dominate their market area effectively. Entrepreneurs who choose this model must possess strong management skills to oversee multiple locations while ensuring brand consistency across the board. This model is especially popular in sectors like food and beverage and health and fitness, where brand loyalty can lead to increased customer retention.

In addition to these traditional models, there are innovative approaches emerging in the franchising space, such as home-based and technology-focused franchises. Home-based franchises offer flexibility and lower overhead costs, making them attractive for entrepreneurs seeking work-life balance. On the other hand, technology and e-commerce franchising models have gained traction due to the increasing reliance on digital platforms. These models often include online retail, subscription services, or tech support franchises, catering to the evolving needs of consumers and the digital marketplace.

As the franchising landscape continues to evolve, it's essential for potential franchisees to conduct thorough research and understand the nuances of each model. Factors such as initial investment, ongoing fees, territorial rights, and operational support vary significantly across different franchising types. By taking the time to evaluate the strengths and weaknesses of each model, entrepreneurs and investors can make informed decisions that align with their business goals and market trends, ultimately positioning themselves for success in the competitive world of retail franchising.

The Evolution of Retail Franchising

The evolution of retail franchising has been marked by significant transformations that reflect changing consumer behaviors, technological advancements, and market demands. The concept of franchising, which allows individuals to operate a business under an established brand, gained momentum in the mid-20th century. Initially, it was primarily associated with the food and beverage industry, exemplified by the rapid expansion of fast-food chains. This early model showcased the potential for franchising to provide entrepreneurs with a proven business framework, enabling them to replicate successful business models in various locations while benefiting from brand recognition.

As the franchise model matured, new sectors began to embrace franchising as a viable business strategy. The health and fitness industry emerged as a notable example, with gym franchises and wellness centers catering to a growing awareness of health and lifestyle. These franchises not only capitalized on the increasing demand for fitness solutions but also provided franchisees with comprehensive training and support, which were crucial for their success. This diversification of franchising sectors illustrated its adaptability and the ability to respond to evolving consumer preferences.

The rise of technology and e-commerce further revolutionized retail franchising. With the advent of online shopping, traditional brick-and-mortar franchises began incorporating digital strategies to enhance customer engagement and streamline operations. Franchises in sectors such as retail and service-based businesses found new opportunities to reach customers through online platforms, expanding their market reach while maintaining the core principles of franchising. This integration of technology not only improved operational efficiency but also opened doors for home-based franchises, allowing entrepreneurs to start businesses with lower overhead costs.

Education and tutoring franchising is another sector that has experienced remarkable growth, driven by the increasing emphasis on lifelong learning and skill development. Franchise models in this niche offer standardized curriculum and support systems, making it easier for franchisees to deliver quality education. This focus on education reflects a broader trend where franchising is no longer limited to traditional sectors; instead, it has expanded into diverse areas such as pet care and real estate, catering to specific needs within the community.

The future of retail franchising is poised for continuous evolution, influenced by changing demographics and global economic trends. As consumer expectations evolve, franchisors must adapt their models to incorporate sustainable practices, personalized customer experiences, and innovative service delivery methods. Investors and entrepreneurs looking to enter the franchising landscape will find a dynamic environment that promises growth and opportunity. By understanding the historical context and the trajectory of franchising, stakeholders can better navigate the complexities of this ever-changing industry, positioning themselves for success in the retail revolution.

Key Trends Shaping the Future

The retail landscape is undergoing a profound transformation driven by several key trends that will shape the future of franchising across various sectors. One of the most significant trends is the increasing integration of technology in retail operations. Entrepreneurs and investors must recognize how advancements such as artificial intelligence, machine learning, and data analytics are optimizing inventory management, enhancing customer experiences, and streamlining operations. Franchises that harness these technologies can gain a competitive edge by making data-driven decisions that improve efficiency and responsiveness to market demands.

Another trend influencing the future of retail franchising is the growing consumer preference for sustainability and ethical practices. Businesses that prioritize environmentally friendly products and practices are not only appealing to eco-conscious consumers but also enhancing their brand loyalty. Entrepreneurs looking to establish or invest in franchises should consider how sustainability can be integrated into their business models, from sourcing ingredients in food and beverage franchises to implementing energy-efficient practices in service-based franchising. This shift towards sustainability is not just a trend; it represents a fundamental change in consumer expectations.

The rise of e-commerce is also reshaping the retail environment, leading to an omnichannel approach that combines online and offline experiences. Consumers now expect seamless interactions between digital platforms and physical stores, making it essential for franchisors to develop strategies that integrate both channels effectively. This is particularly relevant for sectors like health and fitness franchising, where online classes and digital memberships can complement physical locations. Entrepreneurs must embrace technology to create a cohesive brand experience that meets the evolving needs of consumers.

Additionally, the demand for personalized consumer experiences is becoming increasingly prominent. Franchises that leverage customer data to tailor offerings and communications can significantly enhance customer satisfaction and loyalty. This trend is evident in various sectors, including education and tutoring franchising, where personalized learning plans can lead to better student outcomes. Business leaders should invest in customer relationship management systems and tools that allow for targeted marketing, ensuring their franchises remain relevant and appealing in a competitive marketplace.

Lastly, the shift towards remote work and flexible service offerings is creating new opportunities for home-based and service-based franchising. As more individuals seek work-life balance and alternative income streams, business models that allow for remote operations are gaining traction. Entrepreneurs should explore how they can adapt their franchises to accommodate this trend, whether through virtual services, online consultations, or home-based operations. By aligning with the changing workforce dynamics, franchisors can tap into a growing market of aspiring business owners and consumers looking for convenience and flexibility in their purchasing decisions.

Chapter 2: Food and Beverage Franchising

02

Market Overview and Opportunities

The retail franchising landscape is undergoing a significant transformation, driven by evolving consumer preferences, technological advancements, and shifts in economic conditions. Entrepreneurs and investors seeking to navigate this dynamic environment must understand the current market trends and the opportunities they present. The rise of e-commerce has reshaped customer expectations, emphasizing convenience and personalized experiences. As a result, franchises that effectively integrate technology into their business models are positioned to capture a larger share of the market. This includes leveraging data analytics for targeted marketing, enhancing online shopping platforms, and improving supply chain efficiencies.

In the food and beverage sector, health-conscious consumer behavior is paving the way for innovative franchising opportunities. Fast-casual dining establishments that offer organic, locally-sourced ingredients have gained popularity, while plant-based and alternative protein options are increasingly in demand. Entrepreneurs looking to invest in food and beverage franchising should consider concepts that align with these trends, as they cater to the growing base of health-conscious consumers. Additionally, convenience stores and quick-service restaurants that provide delivery and takeout options are capitalizing on the shift toward on-the-go dining, making them attractive franchises for investors.

Health and fitness franchising is another area ripe for growth, fueled by a heightened focus on wellness and self-care. The COVID-19 pandemic has accelerated the trend of remote fitness solutions, leading to a surge in demand for virtual training and mobile fitness apps. Franchise models that combine traditional gym facilities with innovative technology, such as on-demand classes and personalized fitness programs, are meeting the needs of today's consumers. Moreover, specialized training studios focusing on niche markets like yoga, pilates, or high-intensity interval training are also gaining traction, providing diverse options for potential franchisees.

The service-based franchising model is evolving as well, with a growing emphasis on convenience and accessibility. Home-based franchises have become particularly appealing, offering low overhead costs and flexible working conditions. Opportunities in pet care services, home maintenance, and personal care are expanding, as consumers increasingly prioritize convenience in their daily lives. Entrepreneurs can tap into these markets by investing in franchises that provide essential services within their communities, fulfilling a demand that has only intensified in recent years.

Lastly, education and tutoring franchising is experiencing a renaissance, driven by the ongoing need for supplementary education and skills development. As the job market continues to evolve, parents are seeking additional learning resources for their children, creating a lucrative opportunity for franchisors in this space. Concepts that provide innovative learning experiences, such as STEM-focused programs or language acquisition, are particularly attractive. Additionally, technology and e-commerce franchising are reshaping the retail landscape, allowing entrepreneurs to reach broader audiences while minimizing traditional brick-and-mortar costs. By recognizing these market trends and opportunities, investors and business leaders can position themselves for success in the ever-evolving world of retail franchising.

Successful Franchise Models in Food and Beverage

Successful franchise models in the food and beverage sector have become cornerstones of the retail landscape, demonstrating resilience and adaptability in a rapidly changing market. These franchise systems have evolved to meet consumer demands for convenience, quality, and innovation. Entrepreneurs and investors looking to enter this space can glean valuable insights from existing models that have thrived by leveraging brand recognition, operational efficiencies, and customer loyalty. By examining these successful franchises, one can identify key strategies that contribute to their sustainability and growth.

One notable franchise model is the fast-casual dining segment, which merges the speed of fast food with the quality of casual dining. Brands like Chipotle and Panera Bread have successfully carved out niches by emphasizing fresh, high-quality ingredients and customizable menu options. This model appeals to health-conscious consumers seeking quick meal solutions without sacrificing quality. The emphasis on transparency regarding ingredient sourcing and preparation methods resonates well with today's consumers, who are increasingly aware of their food choices. Such attributes not only enhance customer satisfaction but also foster brand loyalty, crucial for long-term success in the competitive food and beverage market.

Another successful franchise model is the coffee shop segment, exemplified by brands like Starbucks and Dunkin'. These franchises have established strong community ties and a unique customer experience that extends beyond just selling coffee. By creating a welcoming atmosphere, they have transformed their outlets into social hubs where customers can work, meet, or relax. The integration of technology, such as mobile ordering and loyalty programs, has further streamlined the customer experience, making it easier for consumers to engage with the brand. For aspiring franchisees, understanding the importance of building a strong brand presence and community connection can be instrumental in replicating this model's success.

Health and wellness-themed franchises are also gaining traction, catering to the growing demand for healthier food options. Brands such as Smoothie King and Freshii focus on nutritious offerings that align with contemporary lifestyle trends. These franchises often capitalize on the rising interest in fitness and well-being, positioning themselves as essential components of a healthy lifestyle. This model not only meets consumer needs but also allows franchisees to tap into a burgeoning market. Entrepreneurs interested in this space should consider how to effectively market health benefits while maintaining a strong, recognizable brand.

Lastly, the rise of technology and e-commerce has led to innovative food and beverage franchise models that transcend traditional storefronts. Ghost kitchens and delivery-only concepts have emerged as efficient solutions to meet the demands of the modern consumer who prioritizes convenience. Brands like Reef Technology have pioneered this model, allowing entrepreneurs to operate without the overhead costs associated with traditional restaurants. This trend highlights the importance of adaptability in the franchising landscape, as successful models embrace technology to enhance operational efficiency and customer engagement. For investors, this represents an opportunity to explore new avenues within the food and beverage sector that align with evolving consumer preferences.

Challenges and Solutions in the Food Sector

The food sector faces numerous challenges that can significantly impact the success of franchises. Fluctuating supply chain issues, such as the rising costs of ingredients and transportation, create uncertainties that can strain profit margins. Additionally, regulatory compliance, including food safety standards and labeling requirements, poses a significant challenge for franchise operators who must navigate complex local, state, and federal laws. This complexity can be particularly daunting for new franchisees who may not have the experience to manage these issues effectively. Moreover, consumer preferences are continually evolving, with a growing demand for health-conscious, sustainable, and locally sourced options, requiring businesses to adapt quickly to maintain relevance in a competitive market.

To address these challenges, food franchises must prioritize establishing robust supply chain partnerships. By collaborating closely with suppliers, franchisees can negotiate favorable terms and ensure consistent access to high-quality ingredients. Additionally, diversifying suppliers can mitigate the risks associated with reliance on a single source, allowing businesses to maintain stability in their operations. Implementing technology solutions, such as inventory management systems and demand forecasting tools, can also help franchisees better predict fluctuations in supply needs and reduce waste, ultimately enhancing profitability.

Regulatory compliance can be streamlined through the development of comprehensive training programs for employees. These programs should focus on food safety protocols, proper handling procedures, and the importance of adhering to local regulations. By equipping staff with the necessary knowledge and skills, franchises can minimize the risk of non-compliance and foster a culture of accountability. Furthermore, leveraging technology to monitor compliance through digital checklists and automated reporting can provide franchise owners with peace of mind while ensuring that all operations meet mandated standards.

Adapting to changing consumer preferences requires a proactive approach to menu development and marketing strategies. Franchises should invest in market research to understand current trends and consumer demands better. By incorporating health-conscious and sustainable options into their offerings, businesses can attract a broader customer base. Additionally, engaging with customers through social media and loyalty programs allows franchises to gather feedback and tailor their services accordingly, enhancing customer satisfaction and retention.

Lastly, fostering a culture of innovation within the franchise can help address the challenges of the food sector. Encouraging franchisees to share best practices, experiment with new concepts, and collaborate on marketing initiatives can lead to a more agile business model. Establishing partnerships with local producers and health-oriented brands can also create unique selling propositions, setting franchises apart in a crowded marketplace. By embracing these solutions, food franchises can navigate challenges effectively and position themselves for long-term success in the evolving retail landscape.

03

Chapter 3: Health and Fitness Franchising

Rise of Health Consciousness

The rise of health consciousness has fundamentally transformed consumer behavior and expectations across various retail sectors, particularly in food and beverage franchising. Increasing awareness of the health impacts of dietary choices has propelled consumers to seek out products that align with their wellness goals. This shift is not merely a trend; it reflects a broader societal movement towards healthier lifestyles, driven by a combination of information accessibility, social media influence, and changing demographics. Entrepreneurs and franchise investors must recognize this evolution and adapt their offerings to meet the growing demand for health-oriented products and services.

In food and beverage franchising, the demand for healthier options has led to a proliferation of brands dedicated to organic, plant-based, gluten-free, and low-calorie products. Fast-casual dining establishments are increasingly incorporating clean eating principles into their menus, while traditional fast-food chains are expanding their offerings to include healthier alternatives. This evolution presents a significant opportunity for franchisees to capitalize on the health trend by aligning their business models with consumer preferences and differentiating themselves in a crowded marketplace.

The ability to provide transparency about ingredient sourcing and nutritional value is becoming a critical factor in attracting health-conscious consumers.

The health and fitness franchising sector is also experiencing a surge in interest, driven by an increasing focus on physical well-being. Fitness franchises that offer specialized classes, personalized training, and innovative workout methods are thriving as individuals prioritize their health. Entrepreneurs looking to enter this market should consider the importance of community building and fostering a supportive environment, which resonates with consumers seeking motivation and accountability. The integration of technology, such as fitness apps and wearable devices, further enhances the consumer experience and drives engagement, providing additional avenues for franchise growth.

Beyond food and fitness, the rise of health consciousness is impacting service-based and home-based franchising as well. Businesses that promote wellness through holistic services, such as yoga studios, nutritional counseling, and mental health services, are gaining traction. Consumers are increasingly valuing experiences that contribute to their overall well-being, leading to a demand for services that support physical, emotional, and mental health. Entrepreneurs venturing into these niches have the opportunity to create meaningful connections with their clients, fostering loyalty and repeat business through an authentic commitment to health and wellness.

As health consciousness permeates various sectors, technology and e-commerce franchising are also adapting to these changes. Online platforms that facilitate the purchase of health-related products, meal kits, and fitness subscriptions are witnessing significant growth. This trend highlights the importance of leveraging digital channels to reach health-focused consumers effectively. Entrepreneurs must not only embrace the digital transformation but also ensure that their online offerings reflect the values of transparency, sustainability, and health. The rise of health consciousness presents a unique opportunity for franchisors and franchisees alike to innovate and thrive in a landscape increasingly shaped by consumer priorities around health and wellness.

Popular Franchise Options in Health and Fitness

In the evolving landscape of health and fitness, franchising has emerged as a formidable avenue for entrepreneurs looking to capitalize on the growing demand for wellness solutions. The health and fitness sector has seen a surge in consumer interest, driven by an increasing focus on personal health, fitness, and overall well-being. As a result, a variety of franchise options have become available, catering to different segments of this market. From traditional gyms to specialized studios, the diversity of franchise offerings allows investors to find opportunities that align with their interests, expertise, and financial goals.
One of the most popular franchise options in this sector is the gym and fitness center model. Established brands such as Anytime Fitness and Planet Fitness have successfully created a widespread presence by offering accessible memberships and a range of workout options. These franchises often appeal to a broad demographic, from casual gym-goers to serious fitness enthusiasts, making them attractive to investors seeking to tap into a large customer base. The relatively low overhead costs associated with these franchises, coupled with their scalability, further enhance their appeal.
Another growing niche within health and fitness franchising is the boutique fitness studio model. Brands like OrangeTheory Fitness and Pure Barre focus on specific workout styles, such as high-intensity interval training or barre workouts, providing a unique selling proposition that attracts dedicated clientele. These studios often foster a strong community atmosphere, which can lead to high member retention rates. Entrepreneurs interested in this segment can benefit from the trend toward personalized fitness experiences, with many consumers willing to pay premium prices for specialized classes and expert instruction.
Health-oriented food franchises are also gaining traction as consumers increasingly prioritize nutrition alongside fitness. Franchises such as Smoothie King and Freshii have successfully merged the health food movement with the convenience of fast-casual dining. These franchises not only cater to health-conscious consumers but also align well with the overall wellness trend. Entrepreneurs exploring this niche can find opportunities in providing nutritious meal options, supplements, and snacks that complement fitness regimes, thereby diversifying their revenue streams.
Lastly, technology-driven fitness solutions are reshaping the industry and providing new franchise opportunities. Companies like F45 Training and Peloton have leveraged technology to create innovative fitness experiences, including virtual classes and personalized training programs. This tech-centric approach appeals to a digitally savvy consumer base that values convenience and flexibility. Entrepreneurs looking to invest in this segment should consider the integration of technology into their offerings, whether through apps, online training, or fitness tracking systems, as these elements are increasingly becoming essential in the modern fitness experience.

Navigating Regulatory Frameworks

Navigating regulatory frameworks is a critical endeavor for entrepreneurs and investors in the franchising sector, especially given the diverse nature of the industry. Each niche, whether it be food and beverage, health and fitness, or technology and e-commerce, has specific regulations that govern operations. Understanding these regulations is essential for compliance and can significantly impact the business's success. Familiarity with local, state, and federal laws, as well as industry-specific guidelines, is crucial for minimizing legal risks and ensuring smooth business operations.

In food and beverage franchising, for instance, adherence to health and safety regulations is paramount. Entrepreneurs must navigate food safety standards, employee health requirements, and local health department inspections. Failure to comply can lead to costly fines and damage to the brand's reputation. Similarly, in the health and fitness sector, regulations regarding equipment safety, facility standards, and certification of trainers are important. Franchise owners must stay informed about the evolving landscape of health regulations to ensure their businesses operate within legal parameters while providing safe environments for customers.

Service-based franchising also presents its unique regulatory challenges. For example, regulations governing licensing and certifications can vary widely depending on the service offered. Whether it's home-based services, tutoring, or pet care, franchise owners must be aware of the specific credentials required in their area. This can include obtaining business licenses, securing professional certifications, and adhering to labor laws affecting hiring practices. By proactively navigating these regulations, entrepreneurs can position themselves for sustainable growth and avoid potential legal pitfalls.

Technology and e-commerce franchising face a distinct set of regulations, particularly concerning data privacy and consumer protection. As businesses increasingly rely on online platforms, compliance with regulations such as the General Data Protection Regulation (GDPR) and the California Consumer Privacy Act (CCPA) becomes vital. Franchise owners must implement robust data security measures and develop transparent privacy policies to safeguard customer information. Additionally, understanding e-commerce regulations related to online sales, shipping, and returns is essential for maintaining compliance and fostering customer trust.

Finally, franchising in sectors like real estate and travel and hospitality also requires careful navigation of regulatory frameworks. Real estate franchisors must comply with licensing requirements, fair housing laws, and disclosure obligations, while travel franchises need to adhere to regulations regarding consumer protection and travel advisories. Each niche within franchising presents its unique complexities, making it essential for entrepreneurs to engage with legal experts and industry associations. By effectively navigating these regulatory landscapes, franchise owners can build resilient businesses that thrive in a competitive marketplace.

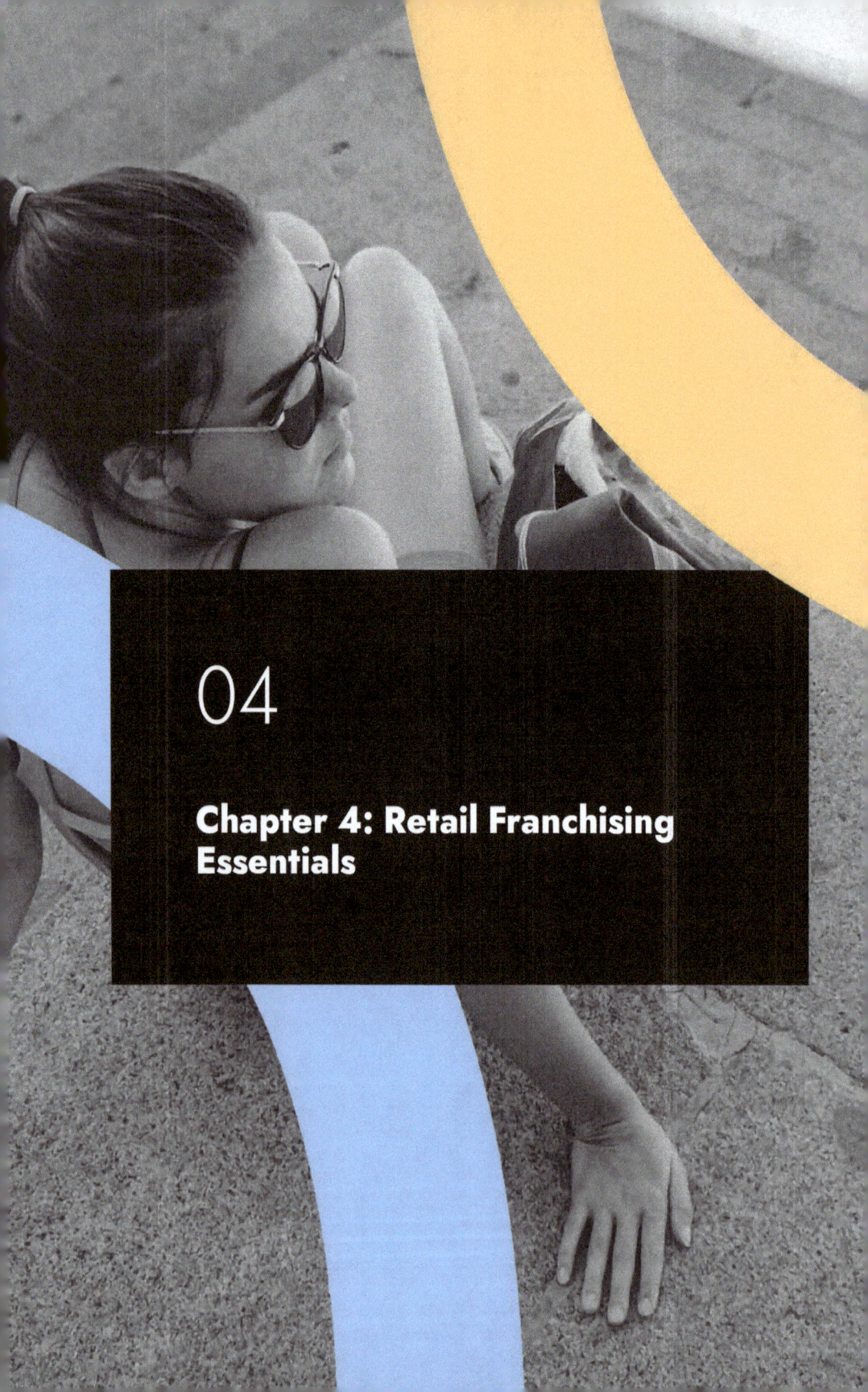

04

Chapter 4: Retail Franchising Essentials

Key Components of a Retail Franchise

In the world of retail franchising, a successful business model hinges on several key components that entrepreneurs, businesspeople, and investors must understand. The franchise agreement is the foundational document that outlines the relationship between the franchisor and franchisee. This legal contract details the rights and obligations of both parties, including the use of trademarks, operational guidelines, and financial arrangements. A clear and comprehensive franchise agreement protects both the franchisor's brand integrity and the franchisee's investment, making it essential for anyone entering the franchising arena.

Another critical component is the training and support system provided by the franchisor. Effective training programs equip franchisees with the knowledge and skills necessary to operate their businesses successfully. This includes initial training on operations, marketing, customer service, and product knowledge, as well as ongoing support that may involve field visits, online resources, and access to a network of fellow franchisees. The strength of the support system can significantly influence a franchisee's performance and, consequently, the overall success of the franchise.

Brand recognition and marketing strategies play a vital role in attracting customers and generating sales. A well-established brand can provide a competitive edge, especially in saturated markets like food and beverage or health and fitness. Franchisees benefit from the franchisor's marketing initiatives, which often include national advertising campaigns, promotional materials, and social media support. This collaborative approach not only reinforces the brand's presence but also drives traffic to individual franchise locations, making effective marketing a key component of retail franchising success.

Financial structure and investment requirements are also crucial elements of a retail franchise. Prospective franchisees must understand the initial fees, ongoing royalties, and other costs associated with running the franchise. A transparent financial model helps potential investors assess the profitability and viability of the business. Additionally, access to financing options, such as loans or franchisor financing programs, can ease the burden of startup costs and allow franchisees to focus on building their businesses rather than struggling with financial constraints.

Lastly, the adaptability of the franchise model to changing market conditions is a significant component of its longevity. In a rapidly evolving retail landscape, successful franchises must be able to pivot and innovate, whether through technology integration, e-commerce expansion, or new service offerings. Franchisors that prioritize flexibility and encourage franchisees to adapt to local market demands will foster a resilient network capable of thriving in diverse sectors, from pet care to travel and hospitality. Understanding these key components enables entrepreneurs, businesspeople, and investors to navigate the complex world of retail franchising effectively.

Finding the Right Retail Franchise

Finding the right retail franchise involves a strategic approach that balances personal passion with market demand. Entrepreneurs must begin by assessing their own interests and strengths. Identifying a franchise that aligns with personal values and lifestyle can lead to greater satisfaction and success. Whether an entrepreneur is drawn to the fast-paced environment of food and beverage franchising or the stability of service-based franchising, understanding personal preferences is the first step in the selection process. This self-awareness will help in narrowing down options and focusing on franchises that resonate on a personal level.

Market research is an essential component in finding the right retail franchise. Entrepreneurs should analyze current trends within various niches such as health and fitness, technology, and e-commerce. Understanding consumer preferences and behaviors can provide insights into which franchises are thriving and which are struggling. Additionally, evaluating the competitive landscape helps potential franchisees identify gaps in the market that they could exploit. This data-driven approach not only informs the selection of a franchise but also aids in making informed projections about its future viability.

Financial considerations cannot be overlooked when choosing a retail franchise. Entrepreneurs must assess the initial investment required, ongoing royalty fees, and potential return on investment. Different sectors, such as pet care or travel and hospitality, can have varying financial models and profit margins. A comprehensive financial analysis, including cash flow forecasts and break-even calculations, is crucial in determining whether a franchise is a sustainable option. Furthermore, understanding the financial health of the franchisor can provide assurance that the business model is sound and capable of providing support throughout the franchisee's journey.

The support and training provided by the franchisor are pivotal in the decision-making process. Franchisees should seek out opportunities that offer robust training programs, marketing assistance, and operational support. Particularly in niches like education and tutoring or home-based franchising, the level of support can significantly influence the franchisee's success. Engaging with current franchisees can yield valuable insights into the franchisor's commitment to helping their partners thrive. This firsthand feedback is instrumental in assessing how well the franchisor supports its franchisees through various challenges.

Finally, entrepreneurs should consider the long-term growth potential of the franchise they are interested in. Evaluating the scalability of the business model and its adaptability to changing market conditions is essential for sustained success. Franchises in sectors such as technology and e-commerce are often at the forefront of innovation, making them appealing options for those looking to invest in future-forward businesses. By analyzing trends, speaking to existing franchisees, and assessing the franchisor's vision, entrepreneurs can make informed decisions that align with their goals and position themselves for success in the evolving retail landscape.

Franchise Agreements and Legal Considerations

Franchise agreements are foundational documents that govern the relationship between franchisors and franchisees, outlining the rights and responsibilities of both parties. These agreements typically encompass critical elements such as the franchise fee, royalties, territory rights, and operational standards. For entrepreneurs and investors, understanding these components is paramount, as they set the framework for the business's operational success and sustainability. Each franchise system has unique requirements, and a thorough review of the franchise disclosure document (FDD) is essential to grasp the expectations and obligations that come with the investment.

Legal considerations play a significant role in the franchise agreement process. Franchisees must be aware of the legal implications related to compliance with federal and state regulations, including those outlined in the Franchise Rule. This rule mandates that franchisors provide prospective franchisees with essential information regarding the franchise opportunity, ensuring transparency and informed decision-making. Additionally, understanding the nuances of intellectual property rights, such as trademarks and proprietary processes, is crucial for maintaining brand integrity and avoiding potential legal disputes. Entrepreneurs should engage legal counsel experienced in franchising to navigate these complexities effectively.

Another important legal aspect pertains to the termination and renewal of franchise agreements. Franchisors typically retain the right to terminate agreements under specific conditions, which may include failure to meet performance standards or violation of operational protocols. Franchisees should carefully analyze these clauses to ascertain the risks involved and the potential financial impact of early termination. Furthermore, the renewal process often presents its own set of challenges, as franchisees may face new terms or changes in fees. Clear understanding and negotiation of these terms can significantly affect the longevity of the franchise relationship.

In the realm of franchising, dispute resolution mechanisms are also critical features of franchise agreements. Many franchisors include provisions for mediation or arbitration, which can provide a more efficient and cost-effective means of resolving conflicts compared to traditional litigation. Entrepreneurs and investors should consider the implications of these clauses, as they may influence their options in the event of a disagreement. A well-structured dispute resolution process can foster a more collaborative atmosphere between franchisor and franchisee, which is essential for long-term success in any franchising venture.

Finally, the importance of ongoing legal compliance cannot be overstated. Franchisees must remain vigilant about adhering to both the terms of their franchise agreements and applicable local, state, and federal laws. This includes staying informed about changes in regulations that may impact their business operations or franchise obligations. Regular consultations with legal experts can help franchisees navigate this landscape, ensuring that they are not only compliant but also positioned to take advantage of new opportunities as the retail industry evolves. A proactive approach to legal considerations can ultimately safeguard the investment and foster a thriving franchise operation.

05

Chapter 5: Service-Based Franchising

Overview of Service-Based Franchises

Service-based franchises represent a dynamic segment of the franchising landscape, characterized by their focus on delivering specific services rather than tangible products. This model appeals to a broad range of entrepreneurs and investors, as it often requires lower initial investments compared to retail franchises. Service-based franchises can cater to diverse sectors, including home services, professional services, and personal care, making them an attractive option for those looking to enter the market with varying expertise and resource levels.

One of the primary advantages of service-based franchises is the ability to operate with reduced overhead costs. Unlike traditional retail stores that require inventory, service-based businesses often rely on skilled labor and specialized knowledge. This allows franchisees to maintain lean operations, focusing on delivering quality services to their clients without the burden of significant stock management. This operational efficiency can translate into quicker profitability, which is appealing to investors looking for a viable return on investment.

Moreover, the flexibility of service-based franchises enables owners to adapt their operations to meet local demand and market trends. For example, a cleaning service franchise can expand its offerings to include eco-friendly cleaning options or specialized services tailored to commercial clients. This adaptability not only helps franchisees stay competitive but also allows for innovation within the franchise model. By responding to consumer preferences and trends, service-based franchises can maintain relevance and drive growth in an ever-changing marketplace.

In addition to operational advantages, service-based franchises often benefit from strong brand recognition and support from the franchisor. Established franchises provide comprehensive training programs, marketing resources, and ongoing support, which can significantly ease the transition for new franchisees. This support network is crucial for entrepreneurs who may be entering unfamiliar industries. Leveraging the franchisor's established reputation can lead to quicker customer acquisition and brand loyalty, reinforcing the franchisee's market position.

Finally, the growth potential for service-based franchises is substantial, driven by changing consumer lifestyles and increasing demand for convenience. As more individuals seek specialized services to save time or enhance their quality of life, the opportunities within this sector continue to expand. Entrepreneurs and investors who tap into the service-based franchise model can position themselves at the forefront of this trend, capitalizing on the evolving retail landscape while contributing to a growing economy that values both expertise and convenience.

Case Studies of Successful Service Franchises

The landscape of service franchising is marked by innovation and adaptability, with numerous brands successfully navigating the complexities of the market. One notable example is the fast-growing franchise of home cleaning services, which has seen a significant surge in demand due to busy lifestyles and a heightened focus on hygiene. Companies that have established themselves as leaders in this niche provide comprehensive training programs for franchisees, emphasizing standardized procedures and customer service excellence. This not only ensures consistency across locations but also fosters a strong brand identity that resonates with consumers seeking reliability in home care.

In the realm of health and fitness franchising, brands like Anytime Fitness have redefined convenience and accessibility. Their model prioritizes 24/7 gym access, allowing members to work out on their schedules. Through strategic partnerships and innovative marketing campaigns, Anytime Fitness has attracted a diverse clientele, from fitness novices to seasoned athletes. Franchisees benefit from a robust support system, including marketing resources and operational guidance, which enhances their chances of success in a competitive industry. This case illustrates how understanding consumer needs and leveraging technology can drive growth in service-based franchises.

The food and beverage sector also showcases successful service franchises, particularly in the coffee shop industry. Brands like Dunkin' have capitalized on their loyal customer base by offering a franchise model that focuses on community engagement and local marketing strategies. Franchisees are encouraged to participate in neighborhood events and collaborate with local organizations, fostering a sense of belonging and brand loyalty. This approach not only boosts sales but also reinforces the franchise's reputation as a community-centric establishment, demonstrating that local integration can be a powerful tool for service franchise success.

In the education and tutoring franchising space, Kumon exemplifies a thriving service franchise that has adapted to changing educational needs. With a focus on individualized learning plans, Kumon franchisees are trained to assess students' unique strengths and weaknesses, allowing for tailored instruction. This personalized approach has resonated with parents seeking effective educational solutions for their children. The franchise's comprehensive training programs and support systems ensure that franchisees are equipped to deliver high-quality educational experiences, illustrating the importance of adaptability and consumer insights in fostering franchise success.

Lastly, the travel and hospitality franchising sector has seen notable success with brands like Hilton Hotels. Their franchise model emphasizes customer experience and brand consistency across various locations, appealing to travelers seeking familiar accommodations. By investing in technology to streamline operations and enhance guest interactions, Hilton has positioned itself as a leader in the industry. Franchisees benefit from a globally recognized brand and extensive marketing resources, which significantly reduce the risks associated with starting a new business. This case study highlights the critical role of brand strength and operational efficiency in the success of service franchises within the travel sector.

Marketing Strategies for Service Franchises

Service franchises require tailored marketing strategies that resonate with their specific offerings and target audience. Unlike product-based franchises, service franchises often rely on personal interactions and customer experiences to attract and retain clients. This necessitates a focus on relationship-building and trust, which can be achieved through community engagement and local marketing initiatives. Franchisees should consider hosting free workshops, informational sessions, or open houses that allow potential clients to experience the service firsthand. Such events not only showcase the service but also help to foster a sense of community and belonging, which is essential for long-term customer loyalty.

Digital marketing has become a cornerstone for promoting service franchises. Establishing a strong online presence through social media, search engine optimization (SEO), and targeted advertising can significantly enhance visibility and reach. Platforms like Facebook, Instagram, and LinkedIn offer unique opportunities for service franchises to engage with potential customers through tailored content that highlights success stories, testimonials, and behind-the-scenes glimpses of service delivery. Furthermore, leveraging local SEO practices ensures that the franchise appears in relevant searches within the community, directing traffic to its website and increasing the likelihood of conversion.

Email marketing remains an effective tool for service franchises to maintain connections with existing customers while reaching potential ones. Regular newsletters featuring promotions, service updates, and educational content can keep the brand top-of-mind among consumers. Personalization is key in this strategy; tailored messages based on customer preferences and past interactions can significantly enhance engagement rates. Additionally, follow-up emails after service delivery can solicit feedback, which not only helps improve service quality but also demonstrates to customers that their opinions are valued.

Franchisees should also consider partnerships and collaborations with local businesses to expand their marketing reach. Cross-promotional opportunities can be mutually beneficial, allowing each business to tap into the other's customer base. For instance, a health and fitness franchise might partner with a local nutrition store to offer bundled services or discounts. Such collaborations can enhance brand visibility and credibility while encouraging potential customers to explore both offerings. Participating in community events or sponsoring local sports teams can further solidify the franchise's presence and commitment to the community.

Lastly, integrating technology into marketing strategies can enhance operational efficiency and customer engagement. Utilizing customer relationship management (CRM) software can help franchisees track interactions, manage leads, and analyze data to refine marketing efforts. Implementing mobile apps or online booking systems can streamline the customer experience and encourage repeat business. Additionally, utilizing analytics tools to assess the effectiveness of various marketing campaigns allows franchisees to make data-driven decisions, ensuring that resources are allocated to the most impactful strategies. By embracing these multifaceted marketing approaches, service franchises can effectively navigate the competitive landscape and foster sustainable growth.

06

Chapter 6: Home-Based Franchising

Benefits of Home-Based Franchising

Home-based franchising presents a unique opportunity for entrepreneurs looking to enter the franchise market with reduced overhead costs and increased flexibility. By operating from home, franchisees can eliminate the substantial expenses associated with traditional brick-and-mortar locations, such as rent, utilities, and extensive staffing requirements. This financial efficiency allows for greater profitability, especially in the initial stages of business development. For many emerging entrepreneurs, this model lowers the barrier to entry, making it an attractive option to invest in well-established brands without the burdensome capital investment typically associated with franchise ownership.

One of the standout benefits of home-based franchising is the flexibility it offers franchisees. Entrepreneurs can tailor their work schedules to fit their personal lives, allowing for a better work-life balance. This adaptability is particularly advantageous for individuals with family commitments or those who wish to pursue other interests alongside their business ventures. The convenience of operating from home also eliminates commuting time and expenses, allowing franchisees to allocate more time and resources to growing their business and enhancing customer engagement.

Additionally, home-based franchising often leverages technology to streamline operations and enhance customer interactions. With the rise of e-commerce and digital marketing, franchisees can easily implement online sales platforms, social media marketing campaigns, and customer relationship management systems without needing extensive technical knowledge. This technological integration not only broadens the potential customer base but also allows for real-time analytics, enabling entrepreneurs to make data-driven decisions that can lead to improved efficiency and profitability.

Home-based franchises also foster a supportive community among franchisees, particularly within established franchise networks. Many franchisors provide comprehensive training, ongoing support, and access to a wealth of resources, which can be particularly beneficial for first-time business owners. This collaborative environment encourages sharing of best practices and strategies among franchisees, which can lead to innovation and improved operational practices. Furthermore, the mentoring opportunities within these networks can serve as a valuable resource for guidance and motivation.

Lastly, the rising trend of remote work and the increasing consumer preference for home-based services highlight the growing relevance of home-based franchising in today's market. As more individuals seek convenience and personalized services, home-based franchises in sectors such as health and fitness, pet care, and tutoring are well-positioned to meet these demands. Entrepreneurs who choose to invest in this sector not only benefit from a scalable business model but also align themselves with evolving consumer behaviors, ensuring their business remains relevant and competitive in the retail landscape.

Popular Home-Based Franchise Models

Home-based franchises have gained significant traction among entrepreneurs seeking flexibility and reduced overhead costs. These models allow individuals to run businesses from the comfort of their homes, making them appealing for those balancing personal commitments with professional ambitions. Popular home-based franchise options span various sectors, including food and beverage, health and fitness, and service-based franchises, catering to a diverse range of interests and skills.

One prominent category within home-based franchises is the food and beverage sector. Companies offering meal preparation, catering, or food delivery services have capitalized on the growing demand for convenient dining solutions. Franchises like meal kit delivery services or mobile coffee shops enable franchisees to tap into the lucrative food market without the need for a traditional brick-and-mortar location. These franchises often provide comprehensive training and support, making it easier for new entrepreneurs to navigate the complexities of the food industry.

Health and fitness franchises also offer lucrative opportunities for home-based operators. With the rise of virtual fitness classes and personal training, entrepreneurs can leverage technology to provide services remotely. Franchises that focus on wellness coaching, nutrition consulting, or online fitness programs enable franchisees to reach clients beyond geographical limitations. This model not only promotes a healthier lifestyle but also fosters community engagement through online platforms, making it an attractive option for fitness enthusiasts.

In the realm of service-based franchising, home-based models excel in providing essential services such as cleaning, landscaping, or home repair. These franchises often require minimal initial investment, making them accessible to a wider audience. With a strong emphasis on customer service and local marketing, franchisees can establish a solid client base while enjoying the benefits of working from home. Additionally, technology integration allows for efficient operations, scheduling, and customer communication, further enhancing the appeal of these franchises.

Lastly, education and tutoring franchises have emerged as a popular choice for home-based entrepreneurs. As families increasingly seek supplemental education for their children, franchises that offer tutoring services, online courses, or educational resources have become essential. These franchises not only provide a rewarding business opportunity but also contribute positively to the community by enhancing learning outcomes. With the ongoing evolution of digital learning platforms, franchisees can create flexible and engaging educational experiences for students, making this niche particularly promising in today's market.

Balancing Work and Personal Life

Balancing work and personal life is a critical consideration for entrepreneurs and business leaders, particularly in the dynamic environment of retail franchising. The demands of running a franchise can often blur the lines between professional obligations and personal time, leading to burnout and decreased productivity. It is essential for franchise owners to develop effective strategies that allow them to manage their time efficiently, ensuring that their business thrives while also maintaining a fulfilling personal life. Achieving this balance not only enhances personal well-being but also positively impacts the overall success of the franchise.

One effective approach to achieving work-life balance is establishing clear boundaries between work and personal time. This can involve setting specific working hours and adhering to them, even in a demanding industry like retail. For instance, entrepreneurs in food and beverage franchising may find it tempting to extend their hours to accommodate customer needs. However, by designating certain times for family, hobbies, or self-care, they can recharge and return to their business with renewed energy and focus. Additionally, leveraging technology can aid in creating these boundaries by enabling better communication and scheduling, thus minimizing work-related disruptions during personal time.

Delegation plays a pivotal role in maintaining balance. Many franchise owners feel compelled to oversee every aspect of their business, which can lead to overwhelming stress. Learning to delegate tasks to trusted team members or utilizing external services can free up valuable time. For instance, in service-based franchising, owners can delegate administrative tasks to support staff, allowing them to concentrate on strategic growth. This not only alleviates the owner's workload but also empowers employees, fostering a more collaborative work environment that can lead to increased productivity and job satisfaction across the board.

Another essential aspect of work-life balance is prioritizing health and wellness. Entrepreneurs in sectors such as health and fitness franchising must lead by example, demonstrating the importance of maintaining physical and mental health. Regular exercise, healthy eating, and sufficient rest are vital. Incorporating wellness practices into daily routines can significantly enhance focus and resilience, enabling franchise owners to tackle challenges more effectively. Furthermore, franchises that promote a culture of health and well-being are likely to attract customers who value such lifestyles, creating a symbiotic relationship between personal health and business success.

Finally, continuous evaluation and adjustment of work-life balance strategies are crucial. Entrepreneurs should regularly assess their commitments and stress levels, making necessary changes to their routines and practices. Engaging in open discussions with family, mentors, or peers can provide valuable insights and support. By embracing flexibility and adaptability, franchise owners can navigate the ever-changing landscape of retail while ensuring that their personal lives remain fulfilling. In doing so, they not only enhance their own lives but also cultivate a sustainable business model that can thrive in the competitive world of franchising.

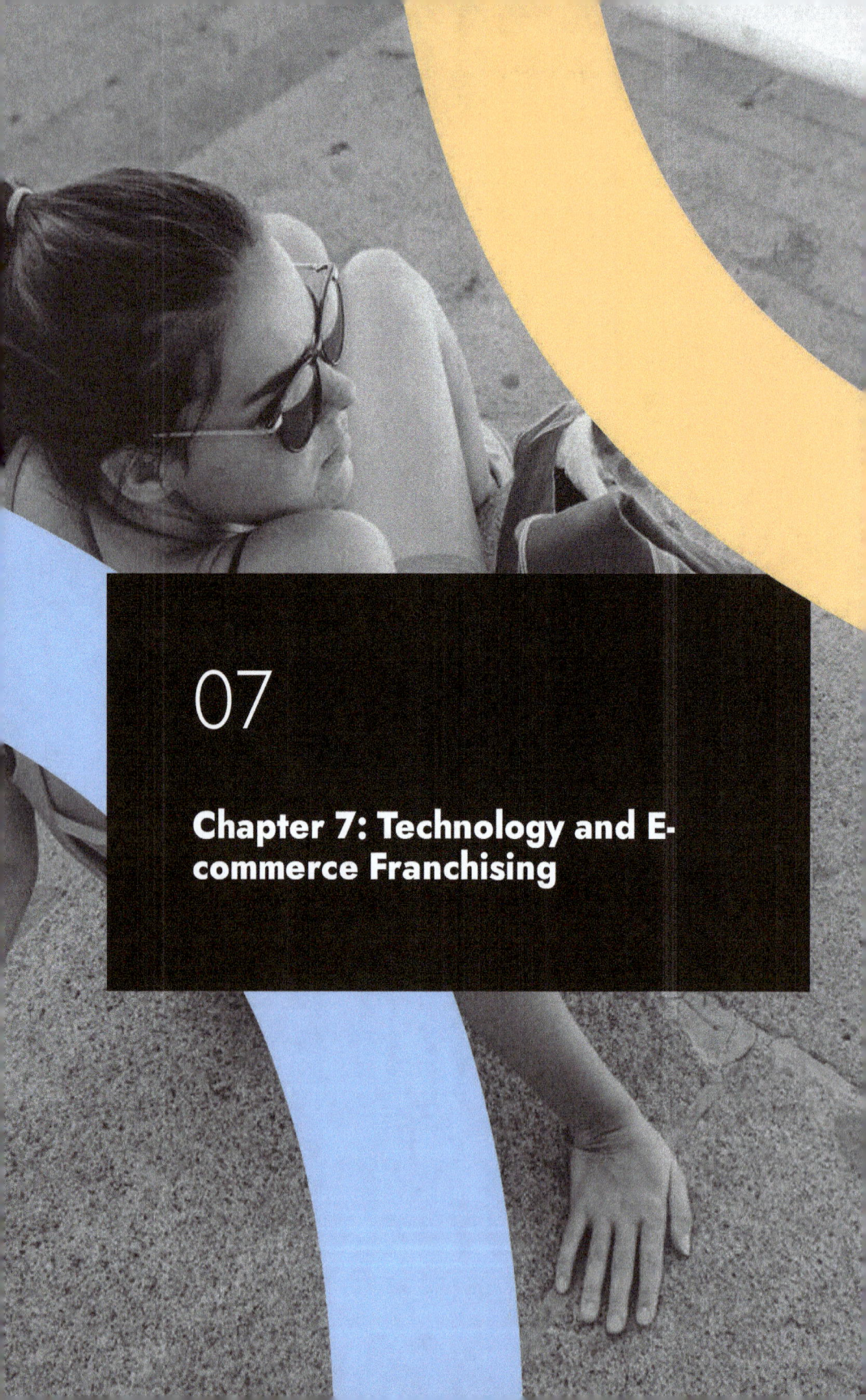

07

Chapter 7: Technology and E-commerce Franchising

The Digital Shift in Retail

The digital shift in retail has fundamentally altered the landscape in which entrepreneurs and investors operate, requiring them to rethink traditional business models and strategies. With the rise of e-commerce and mobile technology, consumers now expect seamless shopping experiences that bridge the gap between online and offline. This shift has prompted franchisors and franchisees alike to embrace digital tools and platforms, ensuring they remain competitive in an increasingly crowded marketplace. For those involved in franchising, understanding and leveraging these digital advancements is crucial to maximizing growth potential and enhancing customer satisfaction. In the realm of food and beverage franchising, for instance, the digital shift has manifested in various ways, from online ordering systems to delivery apps that expand a franchise's reach. Restaurants that once relied solely on foot traffic are now integrating technology to facilitate takeout and delivery services, thereby adapting to changing consumer behaviors. This transformation not only improves operational efficiency but also allows for data collection on consumer preferences, enabling franchises to tailor their offerings and marketing strategies accordingly. As a result, digital tools have become essential for maintaining relevance and driving sales in this competitive sector.

Health and fitness franchising has similarly benefited from the digital shift, with the emergence of fitness apps and virtual training sessions. This has opened new avenues for revenue generation and customer engagement, allowing franchises to cater to a broader audience beyond their physical locations. For instance, gyms and fitness studios are now offering online classes and personalized training programs, which can attract clients who may not be able to visit in person. By embracing technology, these franchises can foster community and loyalty among members, regardless of their geographical limitations, thus enhancing overall brand value.

Service-based franchising is also experiencing significant changes due to the digital shift. Businesses in this niche can leverage online platforms to streamline appointment booking, manage customer relationships, and enhance service delivery. For example, beauty and wellness franchises are utilizing online scheduling systems and customer management software to improve client interactions and operational efficiency. This technological integration not only enhances the customer experience but also allows franchisees to focus on delivering high-quality services rather than being bogged down by administrative tasks.

Finally, the digital shift is equally relevant for industries such as education and tutoring franchising, which are increasingly adopting online learning platforms to reach students. As the demand for flexible and accessible education options grows, franchises that invest in digital solutions can expand their market presence and adapt to evolving consumer needs. By offering virtual tutoring sessions and interactive learning tools, these franchises can cater to a diverse range of learners, positioning themselves as leaders in a rapidly changing educational landscape. Embracing the digital shift is not merely an option; it is an imperative for franchises seeking to thrive in the future of retail.

E-commerce Franchise Opportunities

E-commerce franchise opportunities present a compelling avenue for entrepreneurs looking to capitalize on the expanding digital marketplace. Unlike traditional brick-and-mortar franchises, e-commerce franchises allow for reduced overhead costs and greater flexibility. Entrepreneurs can operate from virtually anywhere, enabling them to reach a global customer base without the limitations of geographical boundaries. This model is particularly appealing in today's fast-paced retail environment where consumers increasingly prefer online shopping due to convenience and accessibility. The ability to tap into established brand recognition while leveraging online platforms positions franchisees for success in a competitive landscape.

In the realm of food and beverage franchising, e-commerce has transformed traditional dining concepts. Many franchises now offer online ordering, delivery services, and meal kits, catering to the growing demand for convenience in food consumption. Franchisees can benefit from well-known brands that have successfully made the transition to online sales, allowing them to attract customers who prioritize convenience and speed. The integration of technology with food services not only enhances customer experience but also streamlines operations, providing a dual advantage for franchise owners.

Health and fitness franchising has also embraced e-commerce, particularly following the pandemic, when many consumers sought at-home workout solutions. Franchise opportunities in this sector now include virtual training programs, subscription-based fitness content, and online wellness coaching. These models enable entrepreneurs to connect with clients in innovative ways, expanding their reach beyond local communities. By investing in health and fitness e-commerce franchises, entrepreneurs can cater to the rising trend of health-conscious consumers while also enjoying the benefits of recurring revenue through subscription services.

In the retail and service-based franchising sectors, e-commerce has introduced new dynamics that enhance customer engagement. Online platforms allow franchisees to showcase their products and services in a manner that is interactive and customer-centric. Entrepreneurs can leverage digital marketing strategies to attract and retain customers, utilizing data analytics to tailor offerings to specific consumer needs. This approach not only drives sales but also fosters brand loyalty, making e-commerce franchises a smart investment for those looking to stay ahead of the curve in retail innovation.

Finally, technology and e-commerce franchising present unique opportunities for entrepreneurs interested in cutting-edge solutions. This niche encompasses a variety of sectors, including education and tutoring, pet care, and real estate, each benefiting from an online presence. By franchising in these areas, entrepreneurs can utilize innovative technologies to enhance service delivery and customer experience. The adaptability of e-commerce models allows for continuous evolution in response to market trends, providing franchisees with a sustainable business model poised for growth in the digital age.

Technology Trends Affecting Franchising

Technology is reshaping the landscape of franchising across various sectors, influencing how brands operate, engage customers, and manage their franchises. The rise of digital platforms has enabled instant communication and streamlined processes, allowing franchisors and franchisees to collaborate more effectively. For instance, cloud-based management systems provide real-time data on inventory, sales, and customer interactions, ensuring that franchisees have the tools they need to operate efficiently. This technological integration not only enhances operational performance but also fosters a stronger connection between franchisees and the central brand, ultimately driving growth.

In the food and beverage franchising sector, technology trends such as mobile ordering and delivery apps have become essential. Consumers increasingly prefer the convenience of ordering from their smartphones, which has led to the adoption of advanced point-of-sale systems that integrate seamlessly with these apps. Furthermore, artificial intelligence is being used to analyze customer preferences and optimize menus, enabling franchises to tailor their offerings to meet dynamic consumer demands. As the competition intensifies, those who harness these technological advancements will likely gain a significant edge in the marketplace.

The health and fitness franchising industry is not left behind, as wearable technology and fitness apps are redefining customer engagement. Gyms and fitness studios are leveraging these tools to create personalized workout experiences, allowing members to track their progress and engage with their fitness community digitally. Franchise brands that incorporate such technologies can enhance member retention and satisfaction, fostering a loyal customer base. Additionally, virtual classes and online training programs have become prominent, allowing franchises to expand their reach and attract clients who prefer at-home workouts.

Retail franchising is experiencing a transformation through e-commerce and omnichannel strategies. With the rise of online shopping, franchises are increasingly adopting integrated systems that allow seamless transitions between physical stores and online platforms. This trend necessitates a strong digital presence, where franchisees can utilize social media and e-commerce tools to enhance their visibility and sales. As retail continues to evolve, franchises that effectively leverage technology to create a cohesive shopping experience will not only survive but thrive in an increasingly competitive environment.

Finally, service-based franchising sectors, including pet care and real estate, are also benefiting from technology. Innovations such as virtual consultations, online booking systems, and customer relationship management software are streamlining operations and improving customer service. These tools enable franchisees to manage their client interactions more effectively, fostering a better experience for customers. As technology continues to advance, the ability to adapt and implement these trends will be crucial for franchise brands aiming to stay relevant and competitive in their respective markets.

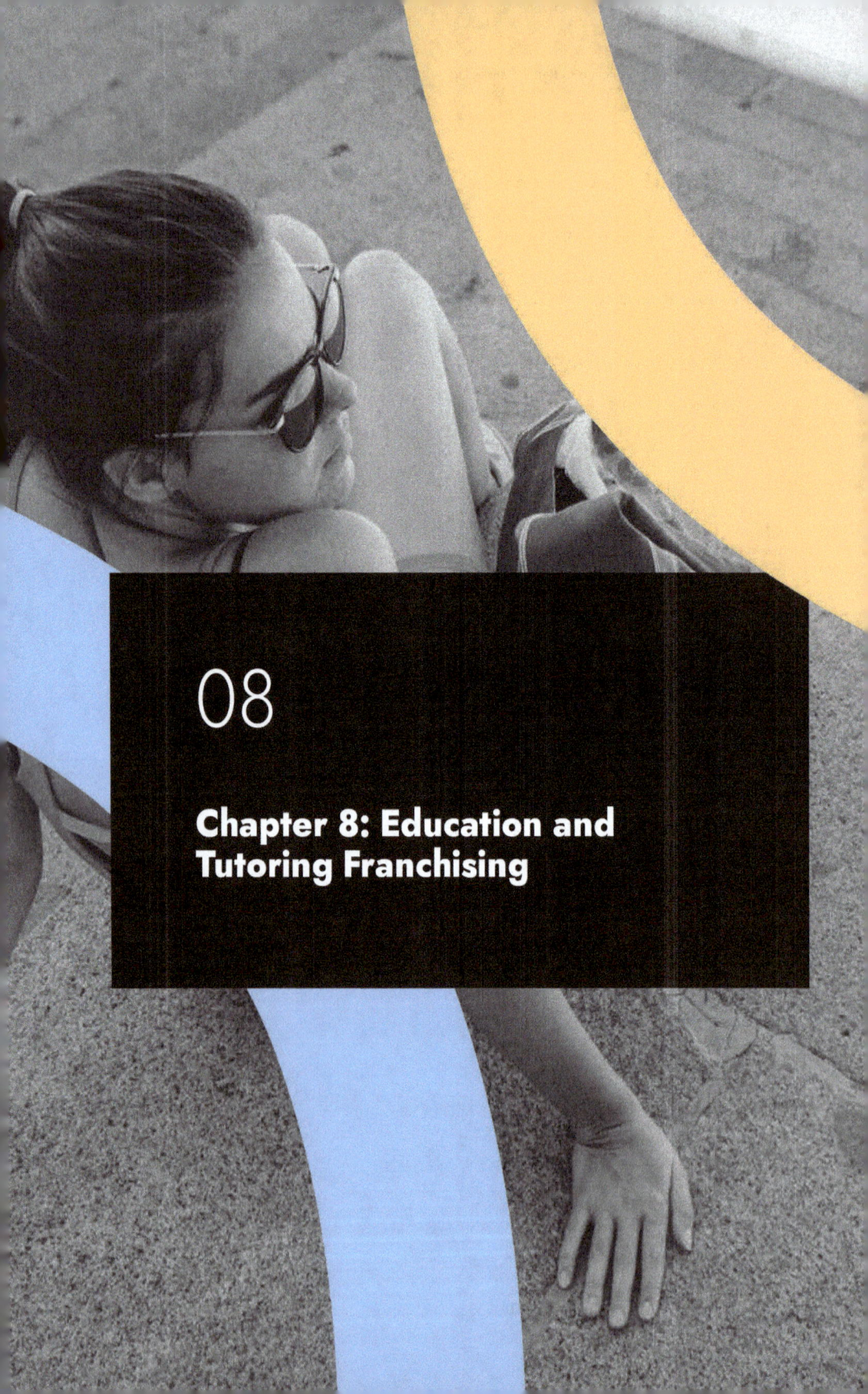

08

Chapter 8: Education and Tutoring Franchising

The Growing Demand for Education Services

The demand for education services is experiencing a significant surge, driven by a combination of societal trends, technological advancements, and an evolving job market. As knowledge acquisition becomes increasingly essential for personal and professional development, entrepreneurs and investors in the franchising sector are recognizing the potential of education and tutoring franchises. This sector not only serves a broad demographic, from children to adults, but also adapts swiftly to the changing landscape of educational needs, making it an attractive opportunity for those looking to invest in sustainable business models.

One of the primary factors fueling this demand is the growing emphasis on lifelong learning. In an era where skills can become obsolete in a matter of years, individuals are seeking continuous education to remain competitive in the workforce. This trend presents a unique opportunity for franchisors who can offer specialized training, certification programs, and skill enhancement courses. Franchises that focus on niche areas, such as coding, digital marketing, or language acquisition, are particularly well-positioned to capitalize on this shift, attracting not only students but also working professionals eager to upskill.

Moreover, advancements in technology have transformed the landscape of education, making learning more accessible than ever. Online platforms and digital resources have democratized education, allowing franchises to reach a global audience with relative ease. Entrepreneurs can leverage e-learning tools, virtual classrooms, and mobile applications to deliver high-quality educational content. This flexibility not only caters to the preferences of modern learners but also reduces overhead costs, making it feasible for franchisees to operate in diverse markets while maintaining profitability.

In addition to individual learners, there is an increasing demand from businesses seeking to invest in the professional development of their employees. Companies recognize that a well-trained workforce is crucial for maintaining a competitive edge. As such, corporate training and educational programs present lucrative opportunities for franchisers in the education sector. By creating partnerships with organizations to provide tailored training solutions, education franchises can expand their client base and enhance their revenue streams, further solidifying their position within the retail landscape.

Lastly, the rise of parental involvement in education has led to a heightened focus on supplemental learning opportunities for children. Parents are increasingly seeking out tutoring services, enrichment programs, and skill-building workshops to complement traditional schooling. Franchises that cater to this demographic, offering personalized attention and innovative learning methodologies, stand to benefit immensely. As the education sector continues to evolve, the growing demand for educational services reflects a broader societal commitment to knowledge and skill acquisition, making it a promising avenue for entrepreneurs and investors in the franchising space.

Types of Education Franchises

Education franchises represent a diverse and dynamic segment of the franchising landscape, catering to a variety of learning needs and preferences. These franchises can be broadly categorized into several types, each offering unique services and targeting different demographics. The most common types include tutoring centers, test preparation services, vocational training, and online education platforms. Each type plays a crucial role in addressing the educational demands of students, professionals, and lifelong learners, making this sector particularly attractive for entrepreneurs and investors.

Tutoring centers are perhaps the most recognizable form of education franchises. They provide personalized learning support for students of all ages, focusing on subjects like mathematics, science, and language arts. These centers often utilize a combination of one-on-one instruction and small group classes to enhance student understanding and performance. The demand for tutoring services has surged in recent years, driven by parental concerns about academic achievement and the increasing competitiveness of college admissions. This trend presents a lucrative opportunity for franchisees looking to invest in a sector with a steady stream of clientele.

Test preparation services represent another vital category within education franchising. These franchises specialize in preparing students for standardized tests such as the SAT, ACT, GRE, and GMAT. With the high stakes associated with these exams, students and their families are often willing to invest significant resources into effective preparation. Franchise models in this area typically offer structured courses, practice tests, and individualized coaching, which not only boost student confidence but also improve test scores. This focus on outcomes creates a compelling business model for investors seeking to capitalize on the education market.

Vocational training franchises are also gaining traction as the workforce demands evolve. These franchises offer specialized training in fields such as healthcare, information technology, and skilled trades. With a growing emphasis on practical skills and employability, vocational training franchises cater to a diverse audience, from high school graduates to career changers. Franchisees benefit from established curricula and industry connections, allowing them to effectively meet the needs of both students and employers. As industries continue to seek skilled workers, the potential for growth in this segment remains robust.

Finally, online education platforms have revolutionized the way knowledge is disseminated and consumed. These franchises leverage technology to provide flexible learning opportunities that can reach a global audience. From language learning apps to professional development courses, online education franchises cater to a wide range of interests and skill levels. The convenience and accessibility of online education appeal to busy professionals and students alike, leading to increased demand for these services. For entrepreneurs and investors, the scalability and low overhead associated with online education make it an attractive option in the franchising landscape.

Best Practices for Managing Education Franchises

Managing education franchises requires a strategic approach that balances operational efficiency with the unique needs of students and educators. One of the best practices involves establishing a robust training program for franchisees and their staff. Comprehensive training ensures that every individual involved in the franchise understands the educational philosophy, curriculum standards, and operational procedures. This alignment not only enhances the quality of education delivered but also fosters a unified brand identity across different franchise locations. Regular refresher courses and updates on educational trends can further equip franchisees to adapt to evolving market demands. Another critical practice is implementing a strong support system for franchisees. This includes providing ongoing assistance in marketing, curriculum development, and administrative tasks. Establishing a dedicated support team that franchisees can reach out to for guidance helps mitigate challenges and instills confidence in their ability to run their businesses effectively. Moreover, creating a centralized communication platform can facilitate the sharing of best practices and resources among franchisees, fostering a collaborative community that contributes to overall brand success.

Quality control measures are essential in education franchising, as they directly impact the reputation and effectiveness of the franchise. Regular assessments and audits can help ensure that each franchise adheres to established educational standards and operational protocols. These evaluations should not only focus on compliance but also on the quality of education provided, gauged through student performance and satisfaction metrics. Implementing a feedback loop where franchisees can report on their experiences and outcomes allows for continuous improvement and adaptation to changing educational landscapes.

Leveraging technology is another best practice that can significantly enhance the management of education franchises. Utilizing learning management systems, online resources, and data analytics can streamline operations and improve the educational experience for students. Franchisees should be encouraged to incorporate these tools into their daily practices to track student progress, facilitate communication with parents, and manage administrative tasks effectively. By embracing technology, education franchises can not only improve efficiency but also align themselves with the preferences of modern learners and their families.

Finally, fostering strong relationships with local communities is vital for the success of education franchises. Engaging with parents, schools, and community organizations can enhance brand visibility and build trust within the community. Hosting events, workshops, and open houses can provide opportunities for franchisees to showcase their educational offerings and connect with potential students. By positioning themselves as valuable resources within their communities, education franchises can cultivate long-term relationships that contribute to sustained growth and a loyal customer base.

09

Chapter 9: Pet Care Franchising

The Booming Pet Care Industry

The pet care industry has experienced remarkable growth over the past few decades, transforming into a lucrative market that attracts entrepreneurs and investors alike. As pet ownership continues to rise, so does the demand for services and products that cater to the needs of pets and their owners. This trend presents a significant opportunity for franchising, allowing business-minded individuals to tap into a sector characterized by its resilience and adaptability. The expansion of pet care franchises offers a compelling avenue for those looking to make a mark in retail, service-based businesses, and beyond.

One of the most notable factors contributing to the booming pet care industry is the changing perception of pets within households. Pets are increasingly viewed as family members, leading to a surge in spending on high-quality food, grooming services, health care, and various accessories. This shift in consumer behavior has created a thriving market where pet owners are willing to invest in premium products and services. Entrepreneurs can leverage this trend by establishing franchises that provide specialized offerings, from organic pet food to luxury grooming salons.

Additionally, the rise of e-commerce and technology has revolutionized the way pet care businesses operate. Online platforms enable pet owners to conveniently purchase products, access subscription services, and book appointments for grooming or veterinary care. Franchisors who embrace digital solutions can enhance their operational efficiency and customer experience, tapping into a broader audience. For investors, this digital transformation represents an opportunity to support franchises that are not only innovative but also capable of scaling rapidly in a competitive marketplace.

Health and wellness trends have also permeated the pet care industry, mirroring the growing awareness surrounding human health. Pet owners are increasingly seeking out services that promote the well-being of their animals, including nutritious food options, exercise programs, and preventive health care. Franchises that focus on these aspects can capture a niche market, providing products such as specialized diets or fitness classes for pets. By aligning with the health and wellness movement, pet care franchises can position themselves as leaders in a sector that prioritizes the holistic care of animals.

Lastly, the pet care industry is not just limited to traditional retail; it encompasses a wide array of service-based opportunities. From pet sitting and dog walking to training and daycare facilities, the scope is vast. As urbanization continues to rise, many pet owners are looking for reliable services to support their busy lifestyles. This trend opens doors for franchising in various formats, including home-based franchises that reduce overhead costs while meeting the growing demands of pet owners. The potential for innovation in service delivery and customer engagement makes the pet care sector an attractive venture for those looking to invest in a thriving industry.

Types of Pet Care Franchises

Pet care franchises represent a dynamic and growing segment of the franchising landscape, catering to the increasing demand for pet services and products. As pet ownership continues to rise, entrepreneurs and investors are presented with numerous opportunities to tap into this lucrative market. Various types of pet care franchises are available, each providing distinct services that cater to the needs of pet owners. Understanding these different categories is essential for anyone looking to invest in the pet care industry.

One of the most prevalent types of pet care franchises is pet grooming services. These franchises focus on providing grooming, bathing, and styling for pets, particularly dogs and cats. The grooming industry has witnessed substantial growth, as pet owners are increasingly willing to invest in professional grooming to ensure their pets' hygiene and appearance. Franchise systems in this category often include mobile grooming options, allowing for convenience and flexibility, which can attract a broader customer base.

Another significant segment is pet boarding and daycare franchises. These businesses cater to pet owners who require temporary care for their pets, whether during vacations or long workdays. Pet boarding facilities offer a safe and nurturing environment where pets can socialize and engage in activities while their owners are away. Daycare services have also gained popularity, as busy pet owners seek out reliable options to keep their pets active and happy throughout the day. Franchises in this niche often provide a range of services, from basic supervision to specialized activities and training.

Pet retail franchises represent another key type within the pet care sector. These franchises typically sell pet food, accessories, toys, and other essential products for pet owners. The rise of health-conscious pet ownership has led to a growing demand for premium and organic pet products, creating opportunities for franchisees to offer unique and high-quality items. Many retail franchises also focus on creating an engaging shopping experience, which can include in-store events, knowledgeable staff, and loyalty programs to foster customer retention.

In addition to grooming, boarding, and retail franchises, there are also specialized pet care franchises that focus on training and behavior modification. These services are essential for pet owners seeking to address specific behavioral issues or train their pets for obedience and agility. Franchise opportunities in this area often encompass both in-person training sessions and online resources, catering to the diverse needs of pet owners. This segment is particularly appealing to entrepreneurs with a background in animal behavior or training, as it allows them to leverage their expertise in a structured franchise model.

As the pet care industry continues to evolve, the variety of franchise options available ensures that there is an opportunity for nearly every entrepreneur. From grooming and boarding to retail and training, pet care franchises offer a plethora of avenues for investment. Each type of franchise presents unique advantages and challenges, allowing potential franchisees to choose a model that aligns with their skills, interests, and market demands. Understanding the nuances of each type can help entrepreneurs make informed decisions as they navigate the future of retail franchising in this vibrant sector.

Customer Engagement in Pet Services

Customer engagement in pet services represents a critical aspect of building a successful franchise in the pet care industry. As pet ownership continues to rise, with millions of households now including pets as family members, the demand for quality pet services has surged. Engaging customers effectively is essential not only for attracting new clients but also for retaining existing ones. This engagement can be achieved through personalized services, loyalty programs, and community involvement, creating a deeper relationship between the franchise and its customers.

Personalization is key in the pet services sector, as pet owners often seek tailored solutions that meet the unique needs of their pets. Franchises can leverage technology to gather data on customer preferences and pet behaviors, using this information to offer customized services. For example, pet grooming businesses can tailor treatments based on the specific breed and health needs of each pet. By providing individualized experiences, franchises can foster loyalty and encourage repeat business, ultimately driving profitability.

Loyalty programs also play a vital role in customer engagement within pet services. By implementing rewards systems that offer discounts, exclusive services, or free products after a certain number of visits, franchises can incentivize customers to return. Such programs not only enhance customer satisfaction but also provide valuable insights into buying patterns, allowing businesses to refine their offerings. This strategic approach to customer retention can significantly boost long-term revenue and create a stable customer base.

Community involvement further enhances customer engagement in the pet services sector. Franchises can host events such as pet adoption drives, educational workshops, or pet health fairs that encourage community participation. These activities not only promote the brand but also demonstrate a commitment to pet welfare and responsible ownership. Engaging with the community helps to build trust and establish the franchise as a go-to resource for pet owners, reinforcing customer loyalty and enhancing the overall brand image.

Finally, effective communication channels are essential for maintaining customer engagement in pet services. Utilizing social media, email newsletters, and mobile apps allows franchises to stay in touch with customers, sharing valuable content, promotional offers, and updates on services. By fostering an ongoing dialogue with clients, franchises can respond to feedback, address concerns, and celebrate customer milestones such as pet birthdays or adoption anniversaries. This proactive approach to communication cultivates a sense of community and belonging, further solidifying the bond between the franchise and its customers.

10

Chapter 10: Real Estate Franchising

Overview of Real Estate Franchise Models

Real estate franchise models have emerged as a prominent segment within the broader landscape of franchising, attracting entrepreneurs, investors, and business professionals seeking lucrative opportunities in a dynamic market. These franchises operate under established brand names, offering a framework that includes marketing, training, and operational support. This structure allows franchisees to leverage a recognized brand's reputation while benefiting from the franchisor's industry expertise. As a result, real estate franchises can provide a comparatively lower risk for new entrants in the competitive property market.

The primary types of real estate franchise models include residential, commercial, and property management franchises. Residential franchises focus on buying, selling, and leasing homes, catering primarily to individual clients and families. In contrast, commercial real estate franchises deal with properties intended for business use, such as office spaces, retail locations, and industrial sites. Property management franchises offer services to property owners, ensuring their investments are maintained and profitable. Each model presents unique challenges and opportunities, allowing entrepreneurs to select an avenue that aligns with their interests and expertise.

Franchise success in real estate often hinges on the support system provided by the franchisor. This includes comprehensive training programs that cover everything from marketing strategies to legal compliance and technology use. Real estate franchisees also benefit from access to proprietary software tools that streamline property listings, client management, and transaction processes. Additionally, ongoing support in the form of marketing resources and networking opportunities is crucial for franchisees aiming to establish a foothold in their local markets.

The real estate market is increasingly influenced by technological advancements, making it essential for franchise models to adapt and evolve. Many franchisors now emphasize the integration of digital marketing strategies, data analytics, and customer relationship management systems to enhance service delivery and client engagement. This tech-driven approach not only helps franchisees to operate more efficiently but also positions them to meet the changing expectations of today's consumers who prioritize convenience and accessibility in their property transactions.

Investors considering real estate franchising should also evaluate market trends, regulatory environments, and economic factors that influence property values. Understanding local market dynamics, including supply and demand, is crucial for making informed decisions. Furthermore, the resilience of the real estate sector, even in the face of economic fluctuations, offers a compelling case for investment. By exploring the various real estate franchise models, entrepreneurs can identify opportunities that align with their goals, ultimately contributing to their success in the retail revolution of franchising.

Market Trends in Real Estate Franchising

Market trends in real estate franchising reveal a dynamic landscape that is influenced by various factors, including technological advancements, shifting consumer preferences, and economic fluctuations. As the real estate market continues to evolve, franchisors and franchisees must adapt to these trends to capitalize on opportunities and mitigate risks. One significant trend is the increasing incorporation of technology in real estate operations. Tools such as virtual tours, advanced customer relationship management (CRM) systems, and data analytics are becoming standard, enabling real estate franchises to enhance client interaction, streamline processes, and improve decision-making.

Another notable trend is the rise of specialized real estate franchises that cater to niche markets. Entrepreneurs and investors are increasingly recognizing the potential of focusing on specific sectors, such as luxury properties, vacation rentals, or commercial real estate. This specialization allows franchises to establish brand authority and attract a targeted client base, ultimately leading to higher conversion rates. Additionally, as consumer preferences shift towards sustainability and eco-friendly practices, franchises that incorporate green building practices and energy-efficient solutions are likely to gain a competitive edge.

The impact of demographic changes is also shaping the real estate franchising landscape. Millennials and Gen Z consumers are becoming a dominant force in the housing market, influencing trends in property types, location preferences, and investment strategies. Franchises that understand the unique needs and values of these generations, such as a preference for urban living and sustainability, can tailor their offerings to meet these demands. Moreover, the growing trend of remote work has prompted shifts in residential demand, with many individuals seeking homes in suburban or rural areas, creating new opportunities for franchises in those markets.

Economic factors, such as interest rates and housing supply, are critical influencers in real estate franchising trends. The current low-interest-rate environment has spurred home buying, making it an opportune time for franchises to expand their services and reach more potential clients. Conversely, rising inflation and potential market corrections could impact purchasing power and overall market stability. Real estate franchises must remain vigilant and adaptable, leveraging market intelligence to navigate these economic challenges effectively. Lastly, the increasing importance of brand reputation and customer experience cannot be overstated in real estate franchising. In a competitive market, franchises that prioritize exceptional service and build strong relationships with clients are likely to succeed. This shift has led to a focus on training and support from franchisors to ensure that franchisees uphold high standards of service. Moreover, leveraging social media and online reviews can significantly impact a franchise's visibility and attractiveness to potential clients. As the real estate market continues to evolve, those who embrace these trends will be well-positioned to thrive in the competitive environment of real estate franchising.

Navigating Challenges in Real Estate

Navigating challenges in real estate can be a daunting task for entrepreneurs and investors, particularly in the dynamic landscape of retail franchising. The complexities of the real estate market necessitate a comprehensive understanding of various factors, including location, market trends, zoning laws, and economic fluctuations. For those involved in franchising, the choice of location can significantly impact the success of a business. A well-situated franchise not only attracts foot traffic but also enhances brand visibility, making it essential to conduct thorough market research and demographic analysis before committing to a lease or purchase.

One prominent challenge in real estate is the fluctuating nature of property values. Entrepreneurs must remain vigilant about market conditions and potential shifts that could affect their investment. For instance, areas that are booming today may face downturns due to economic changes, shifts in consumer behavior, or the emergence of new competitors. Investors can mitigate risks by diversifying their portfolios, carefully assessing each property's long-term potential, and staying informed about local market dynamics. This proactive approach allows them to make strategic decisions that align with their overall business goals.

Another critical aspect of navigating real estate challenges is understanding the legal and regulatory landscape. Zoning laws, permits, and compliance requirements can vary significantly from one location to another, impacting the feasibility of a franchise operation. Entrepreneurs should invest time in understanding these regulations and engaging with local authorities to ensure that their chosen site is compliant. Additionally, seeking legal counsel can help navigate contractual agreements and protect against potential liabilities. A well-prepared franchisee is better equipped to handle any legal hurdles that may arise during the establishment or operation of their business.

Financing is yet another hurdle that can complicate real estate transactions. Securing the necessary capital to acquire or lease a property often poses a challenge for many entrepreneurs. Understanding the different financing options available, including loans, grants, and investment partnerships, is crucial for making informed decisions. Developing a solid business plan that outlines projected revenues and expenses can also aid in attracting potential investors or lenders. By presenting a clear vision and financial strategy, entrepreneurs can improve their chances of obtaining the funding required to secure prime real estate locations.

Lastly, the evolving landscape of technology and e-commerce continues to shape the real estate challenges faced by franchisors and franchisees alike. As consumer preferences shift towards online shopping and home delivery services, brick-and-mortar locations must adapt to remain relevant. This adaptability may involve rethinking traditional storefront models, integrating technology into the customer experience, or even considering alternative location strategies, such as smaller, more flexible spaces. By embracing innovation and staying ahead of industry trends, entrepreneurs in the franchising sector can successfully navigate the challenges of real estate and position themselves for sustained growth in an ever-changing marketplace.

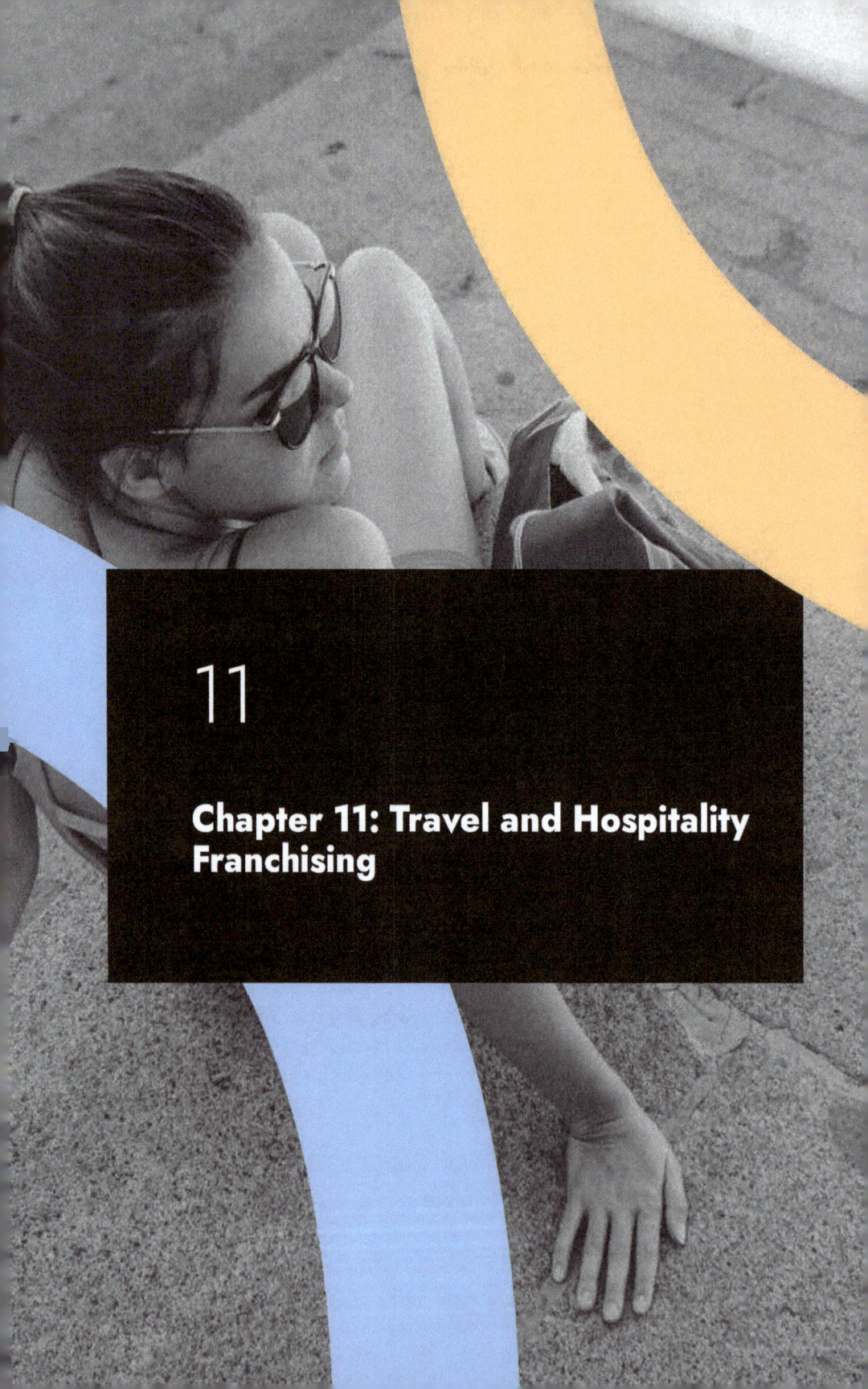

11

Chapter 11: Travel and Hospitality Franchising

Trends in Travel and Hospitality

As the travel and hospitality industry continues to evolve, several key trends are reshaping the landscape for entrepreneurs and investors. One significant trend is the increasing demand for personalized experiences. Travelers today seek unique, tailored adventures that resonate with their individual preferences and lifestyles. This shift has led to the rise of boutique hotels, customized travel packages, and experiential offerings that go beyond traditional lodging and sightseeing. Franchises that can provide personalized services or curate unique experiences stand to gain a competitive edge in this dynamic market.

Sustainability has emerged as a critical focus for the travel and hospitality sector. Consumers are becoming more environmentally conscious and are actively seeking out businesses that prioritize sustainability in their operations. This trend has prompted numerous franchises to adopt eco-friendly practices, from reducing waste and conserving energy to sourcing local products. Investors looking to enter the travel and hospitality franchising space should consider opportunities that align with these sustainability goals, as they are likely to attract a growing segment of eco-aware consumers.

Technology integration is another vital trend impacting the travel and hospitality industry. The advent of mobile applications, artificial intelligence, and contactless services has transformed how businesses operate and interact with customers. For franchises in this sector, leveraging technology to enhance customer experiences is essential. Innovations such as mobile check-ins, virtual tours, and AI-driven customer service solutions not only streamline operations but also cater to the tech-savvy traveler, making it imperative for investors to prioritize tech integration in their business models.

Health and wellness tourism is gaining traction as consumers increasingly seek holistic experiences that promote physical and mental well-being. This trend encompasses a variety of offerings, from fitness retreats and wellness resorts to health-focused travel packages. Franchises that emphasize health and wellness are well-positioned to tap into this growing market, appealing to consumers who prioritize a balanced lifestyle. Entrepreneurs should explore franchising opportunities that integrate wellness concepts into their travel and hospitality offerings, capturing the interest of this health-conscious demographic.

Lastly, the rise of remote work has transformed travel patterns, leading to an increase in longer stays and "workcations." As professionals seek to blend work and leisure, hospitality franchises are adapting their services to cater to this new demographic. This trend presents a unique opportunity for entrepreneurs to develop flexible accommodations and services that support remote workers. By creating environments conducive to productivity while providing leisure activities, franchises can attract a diverse clientele that prioritizes both work and relaxation in their travel experiences.

Franchise Opportunities in the Travel Sector

Franchise opportunities in the travel sector present a dynamic and evolving landscape for entrepreneurs and investors looking to capitalize on the growing demand for travel experiences. This sector encompasses a wide range of franchises, including travel agencies, tour operators, and specialty travel services that cater to various niches such as adventure travel, luxury tourism, and eco-friendly options. The increasing globalization and accessibility of travel have led to a surge in consumer interest, making it an attractive option for those seeking to enter the franchising world. With the right franchise, investors can tap into a market that not only offers substantial financial returns but also aligns with their passion for travel and exploration.

One of the key advantages of investing in travel franchises is the established brand recognition and support that comes with franchising. Franchisees benefit from proven business models, comprehensive training programs, and marketing strategies that can significantly reduce the risk associated with starting a new business. Additionally, many travel franchises offer access to an extensive network of suppliers and partners, which can enhance operational efficiency and provide competitive pricing advantages. This level of support is crucial in a sector where customer satisfaction and service delivery play pivotal roles in business success.

Moreover, the travel sector is increasingly embracing technology, creating a unique opportunity for franchisees to leverage digital platforms for growth. Online booking systems, mobile applications, and customer relationship management tools are transforming how travel services are delivered. Franchises that integrate technology into their operations can streamline processes, improve customer engagement, and enhance the overall travel experience. Entrepreneurs with a background in technology or e-commerce may find particular synergy in combining their skills with travel franchises that prioritize innovation and digital solutions.

Sustainability and eco-consciousness are also becoming significant trends in the travel industry, leading to the rise of franchises focused on responsible tourism. Consumers are more aware of their environmental impact, prompting a shift toward travel options that support local economies and promote sustainability. Franchises that emphasize eco-friendly practices, such as carbon offsetting and partnerships with local communities, are well-positioned to attract a growing segment of socially responsible travelers. Investors interested in aligning their business ventures with ethical practices will find numerous opportunities in this niche.

Lastly, the resilience of the travel sector, even during challenging times such as economic downturns or global crises, underscores its potential for long-term growth. As the world continues to recover from recent disruptions, there is an increasing pent-up demand for travel experiences. Franchise opportunities in this sector not only allow for potential financial success but also enable entrepreneurs to contribute positively to the recovery of the global economy. By choosing the right travel franchise, investors can harness this momentum and create a business that resonates with their values while meeting the evolving needs of travelers.

Managing Customer Experience in Hospitality

Managing customer experience in the hospitality sector is crucial for retaining clientele and ensuring repeat business. In an industry characterized by high competition and evolving consumer expectations, entrepreneurs must prioritize the customer journey from the moment potential guests engage with their brand. This journey encompasses every touchpoint, including marketing, booking, arrival, stay, and post-departure communications. Effective management of these touchpoints can transform a one-time visitor into a loyal customer, ultimately driving revenue and enhancing brand reputation.

One fundamental aspect of managing customer experience is understanding the needs and preferences of the target market. By leveraging data analytics and customer feedback, hospitality businesses can gain insights into what guests value most during their stay, whether it be personalized service, unique amenities, or seamless technology integration. This information enables entrepreneurs to tailor their offerings and create memorable experiences that align with customer expectations, setting them apart from competitors. Fostering a culture of listening and responding to feedback can also enhance the overall guest experience and encourage loyalty.

Training staff to deliver exceptional service is another critical component of customer experience management. Employees are the face of the brand and play a pivotal role in shaping guests' perceptions and experiences. Investing in comprehensive training programs that emphasize service excellence, emotional intelligence, and conflict resolution can empower staff to handle various situations effectively. A well-trained team not only enhances the customer experience but also contributes to a positive workplace culture, which can lead to lower turnover rates and improved service consistency.

Technology plays an increasingly important role in managing customer experiences in hospitality. From online booking systems to mobile apps that facilitate check-ins and service requests, technology can streamline operations and enhance guest convenience. Additionally, utilizing customer relationship management (CRM) systems allows businesses to personalize interactions and anticipate guests' needs. Entrepreneurs should focus on integrating technology that enhances the customer journey while ensuring that it does not detract from the personal touch that is often essential in hospitality.

Finally, measuring and analyzing customer experience is vital for continuous improvement. Collecting data through surveys, reviews, and direct feedback enables businesses to assess satisfaction levels and identify areas for enhancement. Entrepreneurs should establish key performance indicators (KPIs) related to customer experience and regularly review them to ensure alignment with business goals. This commitment to ongoing improvement not only helps in refining the customer experience but also demonstrates to guests that their opinions are valued, fostering loyalty and encouraging positive word-of-mouth.

12

Chapter 12: Financing Your Franchise

Traditional and Alternative Financing Options

Entrepreneurs looking to establish a franchise often face the critical challenge of financing their business. Traditional financing options, such as bank loans and personal savings, remain popular routes for obtaining the necessary capital. Banks typically require a solid business plan, a good credit score, and collateral to secure loans. For many in the franchising sector, especially in food and beverage or service-based franchises, these loans can help cover initial fees, equipment costs, and leasehold improvements. Additionally, personal savings allow entrepreneurs to maintain full control over their business without the burden of debt, though this option is only viable for those who have sufficient savings set aside. In recent years, alternative financing options have gained traction among those seeking to fund their franchise ventures. Crowdfunding platforms enable entrepreneurs to raise funds from a large number of people, often in exchange for equity or future profits. This method allows for a broader reach and can create a community of supporters invested in the success of the franchise. Peer-to-peer lending is another alternative, connecting borrowers directly with individual lenders through online platforms. This can often result in lower interest rates and more flexible repayment options than traditional banks offer, making it an appealing choice for those in fast-growing sectors like technology and e-commerce franchising.

Franchisees can also explore financing through franchisor support programs. Many established franchisors have relationships with banks or financial institutions and can facilitate financing for their franchisees. These programs may include assistance in preparing business plans or negotiating favorable loan terms. Additionally, some franchisors offer their own financing options, allowing franchisees to pay initial fees over time or providing direct loans. This support can be particularly beneficial in sectors like health and fitness or education and tutoring, where upfront costs can be significant.

For those considering home-based or service-based franchising, microloans are another viable financing option. These small loans, often provided by nonprofit organizations or community banks, are designed for startups and small businesses. They typically require less stringent credit criteria and can provide the necessary capital for entrepreneurs to get started without overwhelming debt. Furthermore, grants and competitions specifically aimed at small businesses can provide non-repayable capital to entrepreneurs who meet certain criteria, adding another layer of financial support for those pursuing unique business models.

In navigating the landscape of financing options, it is crucial for entrepreneurs to conduct thorough research and consider their long-term business goals. Each financing route carries its own benefits and risks, and the right choice will depend on individual circumstances, including the type of franchise, risk tolerance, and personal financial situation. By leveraging both traditional and alternative financing options, aspiring franchisees can position themselves for success in the ever-evolving retail environment.

Preparing Your Financial Plan

Preparing your financial plan is a critical step in establishing a successful franchise. It serves as a roadmap, guiding entrepreneurs through the complexities of startup costs, ongoing expenses, and potential revenue streams. First, it is essential to conduct a thorough analysis of the specific franchise model you are considering. Each niche, whether it be food and beverage, health and fitness, or technology and e-commerce, has unique financial requirements and profit potential. Understanding these nuances will help you create a more accurate and tailored financial plan that reflects the realities of your chosen sector.

Start by outlining the initial investment required for your franchise. This should include franchise fees, equipment purchases, inventory, real estate costs, and any other startup expenses. For example, food and beverage franchises may require significant upfront investments in kitchen equipment and compliance with health regulations, while technology franchises might necessitate investments in software and digital infrastructure. Additionally, consider the working capital needed to cover operational expenses during the initial months before the business becomes profitable. A well-documented estimation of these costs will serve as the foundation of your financial plan.

Next, project your revenue streams. Analyze your franchise's sales potential based on market research, demographic data, and competitive analysis. For instance, a retail franchise might benefit from foot traffic and seasonal sales trends, while a service-based franchise could generate income through subscriptions or memberships. It's crucial to create realistic sales forecasts that account for various factors such as location, market saturation, and consumer behavior. This projection will not only help in financial planning but will also be vital when seeking funding from investors or lenders.

Once you have established your initial costs and revenue projections, turn your attention to ongoing expenses. This includes fixed costs such as rent and utilities, as well as variable costs like inventory and marketing. It's important to be comprehensive in this assessment, as underestimating expenses can lead to cash flow issues down the line. Implementing a detailed budget will allow you to track spending, identify potential financial pitfalls, and adjust your strategy accordingly. A solid grasp of your ongoing expenses will enhance your financial stability and provide a clearer picture of your business's profitability.

Finally, prepare for contingencies by including a buffer in your financial plan. The world of franchising can be unpredictable, with market fluctuations and unexpected costs often arising. Having a contingency fund will help you navigate challenges without jeopardizing your business. Additionally, regularly revisiting and revising your financial plan as your business grows will ensure that it remains relevant and effective. By maintaining an adaptable approach, you position yourself for long-term success and resilience in the ever-evolving landscape of retail franchising.

Understanding Franchise Fees and Royalties

Franchise fees and royalties represent the backbone of the franchising financial model, serving as essential components in the relationship between franchisors and franchisees. The franchise fee is typically a one-time payment made by the franchisee upon signing the franchise agreement. This fee grants the franchisee access to the franchisor's brand, business model, and support systems. It varies considerably depending on the brand's reputation, market penetration, and the resources provided to the franchisee. For new entrepreneurs entering franchising, understanding this initial investment is crucial. It not only impacts the startup costs but also sets the stage for the financial obligations that will follow. Royalties, on the other hand, are ongoing payments made by the franchisee to the franchisor, often calculated as a percentage of the franchisee's gross sales. This arrangement is designed to fund continuous support services, including marketing, training, and operational assistance. The royalty structure can vary significantly among different franchises, ranging from a fixed fee to a sliding scale based on sales performance. For business people and investors, analyzing these fees is vital as they can influence profitability and cash flow. Understanding the royalty rate can help prospective franchisees gauge the long-term financial commitment required to sustain the business.

Different sectors of franchising exhibit unique fee and royalty structures. In the food and beverage industry, for instance, franchise fees may be higher due to the costs associated with inventory management and compliance with health regulations. Conversely, in service-based franchising, lower initial fees might be prevalent, reflecting lower startup costs. Each niche, whether it be health and fitness, retail, or technology, has its own cost dynamics influenced by market demand, competition, and the level of ongoing support provided by the franchisor. Entrepreneurs must assess these factors when determining the best franchise fit for their investment goals.

Moreover, the terms of franchise fees and royalties may also include additional costs, such as advertising fees, technology fees, or other contributions to a national marketing fund. These supplementary fees can significantly impact a franchisee's bottom line. It is important for potential franchisees to conduct thorough due diligence, reviewing the Franchise Disclosure Document (FDD) to understand all potential costs associated with the franchise. This transparency can help in making informed decisions and developing realistic financial projections over the lifespan of the franchise.

In conclusion, understanding franchise fees and royalties is integral to success in the franchising landscape. Entrepreneurs, business people, and investors must navigate these financial obligations carefully, as they play a significant role in the overall profitability and sustainability of a franchise. By appreciating the nuances of each franchise's fee structure and aligning their financial strategies accordingly, prospective franchisees can better position themselves for long-term success in their chosen niche.

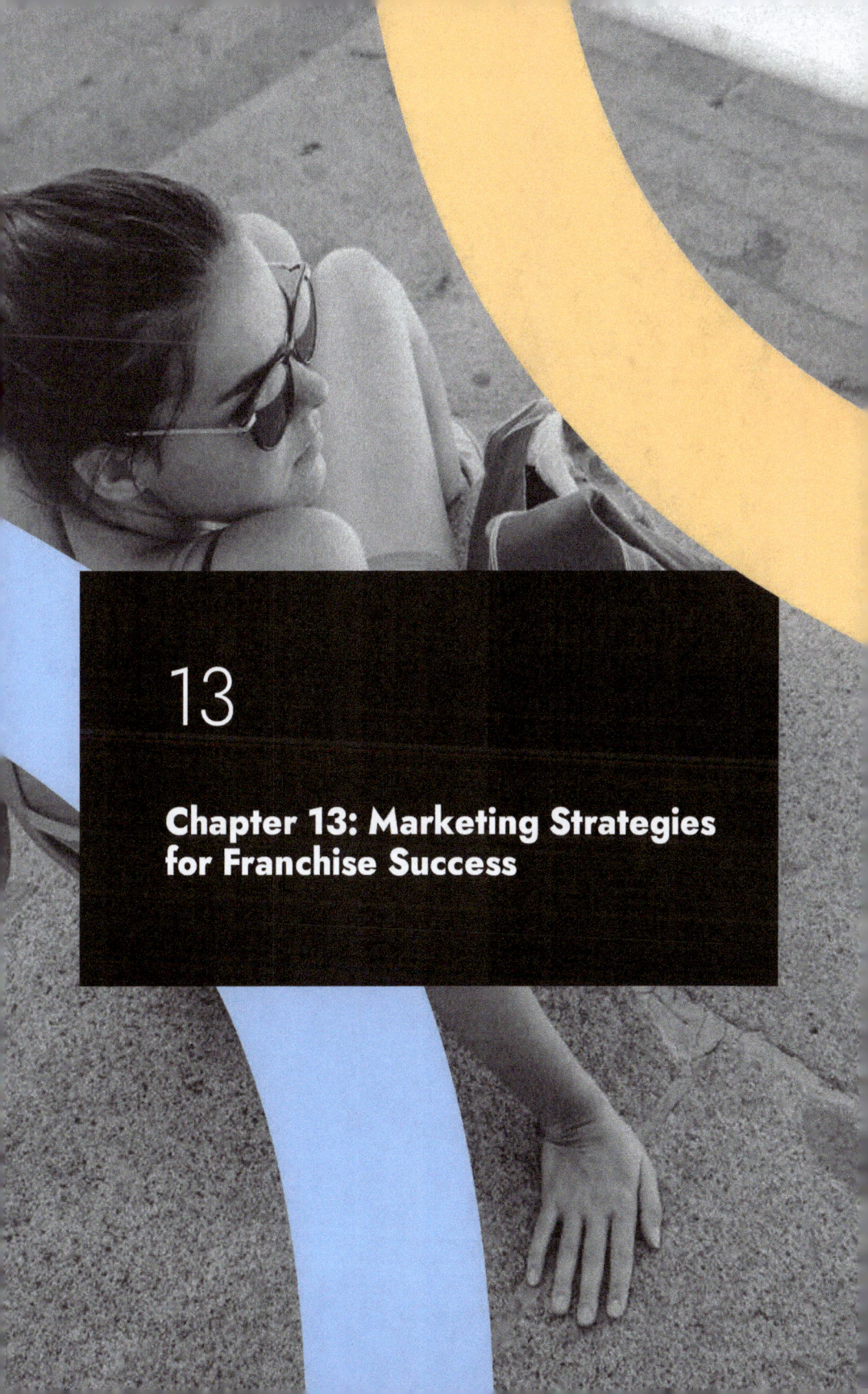

Chapter 13: Marketing Strategies for Franchise Success

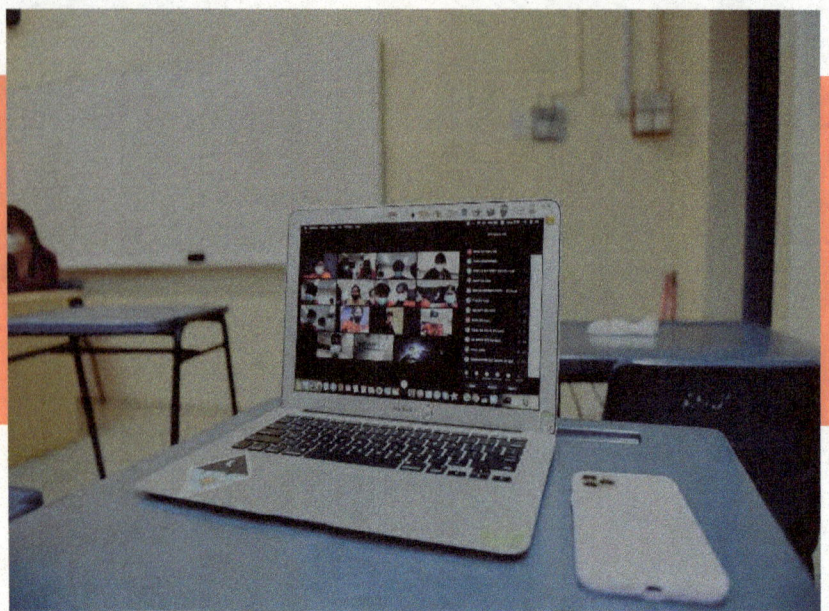

Branding and Positioning Your Franchise

Branding and positioning are critical components in the success of any franchise, as they establish the identity and market presence of the business. A strong brand embodies the values, mission, and vision of the franchise, creating a unique image in the minds of consumers. For entrepreneurs and investors in various niches, including food and beverage, health and fitness, and technology, understanding how to effectively brand and position their franchises can lead to increased customer loyalty and market share. The franchise must communicate its value proposition clearly to differentiate itself from competitors and resonate with its target audience, whether they are seeking a unique dining experience, fitness solutions, or innovative educational services.

To successfully brand a franchise, it is vital to develop a cohesive brand strategy that encompasses all aspects of the business, including logo design, marketing messages, and customer interactions. Entrepreneurs should consider how their brand reflects their franchise's core values and aligns with the expectations of their target market. For instance, a health and fitness franchise might emphasize wellness and community, while a travel and hospitality franchise may highlight adventure and relaxation. Ensuring consistency across all touchpoints reinforces the brand's identity and builds trust with customers, making it essential for franchise owners to maintain brand integrity throughout their operations.
Positioning a franchise involves identifying the niche within the broader market and establishing a clear competitive advantage. This requires a thorough market analysis to understand customer preferences and industry trends. Entrepreneurs must determine how their franchise can fill gaps in the market or improve upon existing offerings. For example, in the pet care franchising sector, positioning as a provider of premium, eco-friendly products can attract environmentally conscious consumers. By defining a unique selling proposition, franchise owners can create a compelling narrative that appeals to their target demographic and effectively communicates why their franchise is the best choice.
Moreover, leveraging digital channels is essential for modern branding and positioning strategies. With the rise of e-commerce and technology, franchises must embrace online marketing and social media to enhance their visibility and engage with customers. Entrepreneurs should invest in a robust online presence, utilizing platforms such as Instagram, Facebook, and LinkedIn to showcase their brand story, share customer testimonials, and promote special offers. Additionally, integrating e-commerce capabilities can streamline the purchasing process and expand the franchise's reach, appealing to a broader audience and driving sales.
Finally, ongoing evaluation and adaptation of branding and positioning strategies are crucial for long-term success. As market dynamics shift and consumer preferences evolve, franchise owners must remain agile and responsive to these changes. Regularly soliciting feedback from customers and analyzing sales data can provide valuable insights into brand perception and effectiveness. By being proactive in refining their branding and positioning efforts, entrepreneurs can ensure their franchise remains relevant and continues to thrive in an increasingly competitive retail landscape.

Digital Marketing Tactics for Franchises

Digital marketing has become an essential component for franchises aiming to establish a strong online presence and engage effectively with their target audiences. In the competitive landscape of franchising, employing a multi-faceted digital marketing strategy is not just beneficial; it is necessary for sustainability and growth. This subchapter explores various digital marketing tactics that can be employed by franchises across diverse sectors, including food and beverage, health and fitness, retail, and more.

One effective tactic is search engine optimization (SEO), which helps franchises enhance their visibility on search engines. By optimizing their websites with relevant keywords, franchises can attract more organic traffic and improve their rankings in search results. Local SEO is particularly crucial for franchises, as it allows them to target potential customers in specific geographic locations. This is especially important for food and beverage and service-based franchises, where proximity often plays a significant role in consumer decisions. Implementing local business listings and Google My Business pages can further enhance visibility in local searches.

Social media marketing is another powerful tool for franchises to engage with their audience and build brand loyalty. Platforms such as Facebook, Instagram, and Twitter offer unique opportunities for franchisors to connect with customers through organic posts, paid advertisements, and promotions. For franchises in sectors like travel and hospitality, visually appealing content showcasing destinations and experiences can drive engagement. Moreover, user-generated content and customer reviews shared on social media can enhance credibility and encourage potential customers to choose their franchise over competitors.

Email marketing remains a cornerstone of digital marketing strategies for franchises, providing a direct line of communication with existing and potential customers. Through targeted email campaigns, franchises can share promotions, updates, and personalized content that resonate with their audience. Segmentation is key here; by dividing their mailing list based on customer behavior and preferences, franchises can tailor their messages to different audience segments, enhancing engagement and conversion rates. This tactic is particularly effective for home-based and education franchises, where personalized communication can significantly impact customer retention.

Pay-per-click (PPC) advertising also plays a vital role in driving traffic to franchise websites. Through carefully crafted ad campaigns on platforms like Google Ads and social media, franchises can target specific demographics and geographic areas, ensuring that their marketing efforts reach the right audience. This tactic allows for measurable results, enabling franchises to analyze performance and adjust their strategies accordingly. For technology and e-commerce franchises, leveraging PPC can help capture the attention of potential customers during critical buying moments, ultimately leading to increased sales.
Incorporating analytics and data-driven decision-making into digital marketing strategies is essential for franchises seeking to optimize their efforts. By utilizing tools like Google Analytics, franchises can gather insights into user behavior, track campaign performance, and identify areas for improvement. Understanding which tactics yield the highest return on investment allows franchises to allocate their resources more effectively. For all types of franchises, from pet care to real estate, leveraging data to inform marketing strategies can lead to more successful outcomes and a stronger market position.

Customer Loyalty Programs

Customer loyalty programs have become an essential strategy for businesses across various sectors, particularly within franchising. These programs are designed to reward repeat customers, encouraging them to return and make additional purchases. By fostering a strong connection between customers and brands, loyalty programs can significantly enhance customer retention, reduce marketing costs, and increase overall profitability. For entrepreneurs and investors in the franchising space, understanding the mechanics of effective loyalty programs is crucial to building a sustainable business model.
In the food and beverage sector, loyalty programs often take the form of points systems or tiered rewards. Customers earn points for each purchase, which can later be redeemed for discounts, free products, or exclusive offers. This not only incentivizes repeat visits but also encourages customers to spend more in order to reach reward thresholds. Successful franchises in this niche have leveraged technology to streamline the process, utilizing mobile apps to track points and offer personalized promotions based on customer preferences. This level of customization can significantly enhance the customer experience and increase brand loyalty.

Health and fitness franchises benefit from loyalty programs that promote not only repeat visits but also member engagement. Programs that reward customers for attendance at classes or completion of fitness milestones can create a sense of community and accountability. By integrating social elements, such as challenges or group rewards, these programs can motivate members to stay committed to their fitness goals while simultaneously boosting retention rates. For entrepreneurs in this sector, understanding the psychological aspects of loyalty can lead to the development of innovative programs that resonate with customers on a personal level.

Retail franchising also presents unique opportunities for loyalty programs, particularly through omnichannel strategies that integrate online and offline shopping experiences. A comprehensive loyalty program can track customer behavior across various platforms, allowing businesses to tailor marketing efforts and promotions to individual preferences. By creating a seamless shopping experience, franchises can enhance customer satisfaction and loyalty. Moreover, data collected through these programs can provide valuable insights into consumer trends, enabling businesses to adapt and remain competitive in an ever-evolving retail landscape.

Service-based and home-based franchises can leverage loyalty programs to build strong relationships with clients. These programs can reward customers for referrals, repeat business, or engagement with services. Personalized communication and follow-ups can enhance customer relationships, making clients feel valued and appreciated. In sectors such as pet care or real estate, loyalty programs can also include educational components, offering clients resources or discounts on additional services. By integrating loyalty initiatives into their business models, entrepreneurs can create a loyal customer base that is essential for long-term success.

Chapter 14: Scaling and Expanding Your Franchise

Strategies for Growth

In the dynamic landscape of retail franchising, entrepreneurs must adopt innovative strategies for growth to remain competitive and relevant. One effective approach is the diversification of product and service offerings. By expanding the range of goods or services available, franchisors can attract a broader customer base and encourage repeat visits. For instance, a food and beverage franchise could introduce seasonal menu items or limited-time offers, while a health and fitness franchise might expand into wellness products or online training programs. This not only boosts sales but also enhances brand loyalty as customers associate the franchise with variety and responsiveness to market trends. Leveraging technology is another crucial strategy for driving growth in retail franchising. The integration of e-commerce capabilities allows franchises to tap into online sales, which can significantly increase revenue streams. Franchises should invest in user-friendly websites and mobile apps that facilitate online ordering and delivery. Moreover, adopting data analytics tools can help franchisors understand consumer behavior and preferences, enabling them to tailor their offerings accordingly. This approach not only meets the demands of tech-savvy customers but also positions the franchise as a forward-thinking brand in a competitive market.

Franchisors should also focus on enhancing customer experience as a primary growth strategy. This can be achieved by training staff to provide exceptional service, using loyalty programs to reward repeat customers, and creating an inviting store atmosphere. In service-based and home-based franchising, personalized interactions can set a brand apart from competitors. For example, a tutoring franchise could implement customized learning plans for each student, while a pet care franchise might offer personalized grooming services. By prioritizing customer satisfaction, franchises can build a strong reputation that drives word-of-mouth referrals and fosters long-term success.

Strategic partnerships and collaborations can also serve as powerful tools for growth. By teaming up with complementary businesses, franchises can expand their reach and enhance their offerings. For instance, a travel and hospitality franchise could partner with local attractions to offer exclusive deals or packages, while a real estate franchise might collaborate with home improvement services to provide added value to clients. These partnerships not only create a more comprehensive service offering but also enhance brand visibility and attract new customers through cross-promotion.

Lastly, continuous training and support for franchisees is vital for maintaining growth across the franchising network. Providing ongoing education on industry trends, marketing strategies, and operational best practices ensures that franchisees are well-equipped to adapt to changing market conditions. Regular communication and feedback mechanisms can foster a sense of community among franchisees, encouraging them to share successful strategies and insights. By investing in franchisee success, the franchisor cultivates a robust and resilient network, ultimately driving collective growth and longevity in the retail franchising sector.

Multi-Unit Franchise Ownership

Multi-unit franchise ownership has emerged as a significant trend in the franchising sector, attracting entrepreneurs and investors looking to amplify their business portfolios. This model allows individuals to own and operate multiple franchise locations under a single brand, providing several advantages that single-unit ownership cannot match. The potential for increased revenue, operational efficiencies, and brand loyalty are compelling reasons behind this shift. For those in diverse niches such as food and beverage, health and fitness, and retail, multi-unit ownership offers a strategic pathway to capitalize on market demand while mitigating risks associated with economic fluctuations.

One of the primary benefits of multi-unit franchise ownership is the ability to achieve economies of scale. Franchisees who operate multiple locations can streamline operations, reduce overhead costs, and negotiate better terms with suppliers. This operational efficiency not only enhances profit margins but also allows for more robust marketing strategies and customer engagement initiatives. For instance, a multi-unit owner in the food and beverage sector can implement cohesive promotional campaigns across all locations, generating a stronger brand presence and customer loyalty. This synergy is particularly beneficial in competitive markets where differentiation is key.

Another critical aspect of multi-unit ownership is the potential for diversified revenue streams. By operating in various niches, such as health and fitness, education and tutoring, or even pet care franchising, franchisees can spread their risk across different markets. This diversification is particularly important in volatile economic climates, where consumer preferences may shift unexpectedly. For example, an entrepreneur with interests in both retail and travel franchising can adapt more readily to changes in consumer behavior by reallocating resources and adjusting strategies based on performance across their portfolio.

The support systems available to multi-unit franchise owners also contribute to their success. Many franchisors provide robust training and resources tailored for multi-unit operators, including advanced management training, operational toolkits, and access to proprietary technology. These resources empower franchisees to manage multiple locations effectively, ensuring consistency in service delivery and product quality. Furthermore, the networking opportunities available through multi-unit ownership can lead to valuable partnerships and insights, further enhancing business growth and innovation.

Investors considering multi-unit franchise ownership should also be aware of the challenges that come with this model. The initial investment can be significant, as franchisees must secure financing for multiple locations, and the demands of managing several operations require strong leadership and organizational skills. However, with thorough research, strategic planning, and a commitment to continuous improvement, entrepreneurs can navigate these challenges successfully. By leveraging the benefits of multi-unit ownership, they position themselves to thrive in the ever-evolving landscape of retail franchising.

Franchising Internationally

Franchising internationally presents a unique set of opportunities and challenges that entrepreneurs and investors must navigate carefully. As the global marketplace continues to expand, many franchisors are looking beyond their domestic borders to tap into new markets. This approach can amplify brand visibility, increase revenue streams, and diversify business risks. However, the complexities of entering foreign markets require thorough research and strategic planning. Understanding cultural nuances, consumer behavior, legal frameworks, and market demands is critical for success in international franchising.

One of the key considerations for franchising internationally is the selection of the right market. Each country has its own economic environment, regulatory requirements, and consumer preferences. Entrepreneurs must conduct extensive market research to identify regions with a strong demand for their products or services. For example, a food and beverage franchise that thrives in North America may face different consumer tastes and dietary restrictions in Asia or Europe. Therefore, adapting the franchise model to align with local preferences while maintaining brand integrity is paramount.

Legal compliance is another vital factor in the international franchising landscape. Each country has specific laws governing franchises, including disclosure requirements, franchise agreements, and intellectual property protections. Franchisors must familiarize themselves with these regulations to avoid potential legal pitfalls. Seeking local legal counsel can be beneficial in navigating the complexities of franchise law, ensuring that agreements are compliant and protecting the franchise's brand and assets in foreign jurisdictions.

Moreover, establishing a robust support system for franchisees is crucial in international markets. Successful franchising relies on effective training, marketing, and operational support. Franchisors must develop comprehensive training programs that account for local business practices and workforce capabilities. This support extends to ongoing communication and assistance, enabling franchisees to adapt to market changes and consumer trends. By fostering strong relationships with franchisees, brands can enhance their reputation and drive growth in international markets.

Finally, technology plays a pivotal role in facilitating international franchising. E-commerce platforms, digital marketing strategies, and advanced supply chain management tools can streamline operations and improve customer engagement across borders. Franchisors should leverage technology to enhance their brand presence and operational efficiency, enabling them to compete effectively in diverse markets. By embracing technological advancements, franchises can not only optimize their performance but also create a seamless experience for both franchisees and customers, ultimately driving the success of their international ventures.

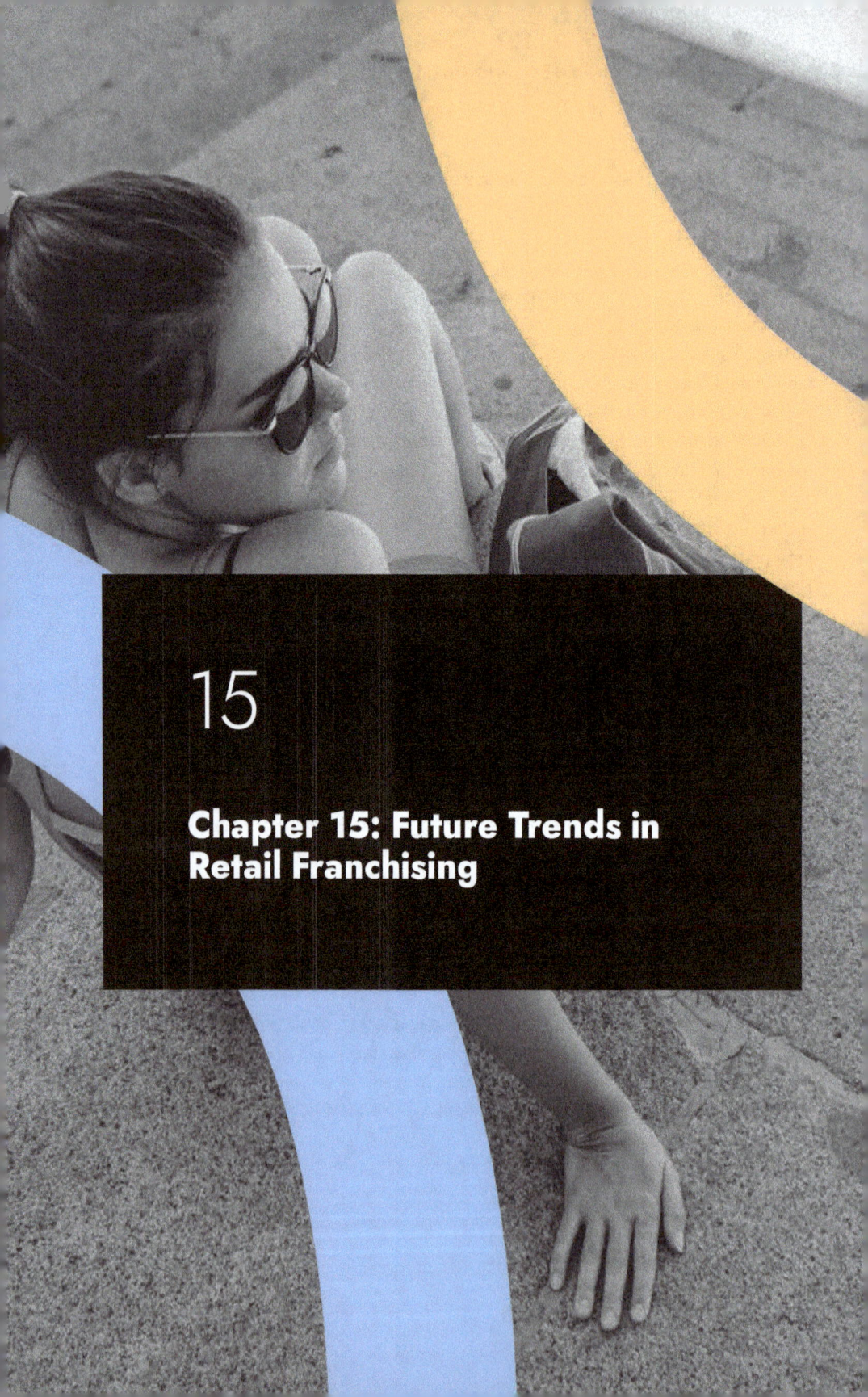

15

Chapter 15: Future Trends in Retail Franchising

Sustainability and Ethical Franchising

Sustainability and ethical franchising are becoming increasingly crucial in today's business landscape, where consumers are more conscious of their purchasing choices and the impact these choices have on the environment and society. Entrepreneurs and investors in various franchising niches must recognize that integrating sustainable practices not only enhances brand reputation but also drives customer loyalty. Franchisors who prioritize sustainability can differentiate themselves in competitive markets, particularly in sectors such as food and beverage, health and fitness, and retail, where consumer preferences are rapidly shifting toward eco-friendly and socially responsible options. In food and beverage franchising, sustainability often manifests in sourcing ingredients locally, reducing waste, and utilizing eco-friendly packaging. This approach not only minimizes the environmental footprint but also supports local economies, creating a win-win scenario for both franchise owners and their communities. Investors looking to enter this space should assess potential franchises on their commitment to sustainable sourcing and waste reduction initiatives, as these factors can significantly influence long-term viability and profitability.

Health and fitness franchising also presents unique opportunities for sustainable practices. Many consumers are increasingly interested in holistic wellness, which includes not just physical health but also mental and environmental well-being. Franchisors in this niche can implement sustainable practices by promoting eco-friendly gyms, using energy-efficient equipment, and offering wellness programs that emphasize mental health and community engagement. By prioritizing sustainability, these franchises can attract health-conscious consumers who value brands that align with their lifestyle choices.

Service-based franchising, including sectors like education and tutoring or home-based services, can also benefit from ethical practices. Franchisors can focus on inclusivity and diversity in hiring, ensuring that their teams reflect the communities they serve. Moreover, implementing transparent business practices and fair compensation for franchisees fosters trust and loyalty. Investors should seek out franchises that prioritize ethical considerations, as these businesses are likely to cultivate strong relationships with customers and franchisees alike, leading to sustainable growth.

Finally, technology and e-commerce franchising present new avenues for promoting sustainability. Brands can leverage digital platforms to minimize resource use, optimize supply chains, and promote products that have lower environmental impacts. A strong commitment to ethical practices in this niche not only appeals to eco-conscious consumers but also positions franchises as leaders in innovation and responsibility. Entrepreneurs and investors must remain vigilant in assessing the sustainability of their chosen franchises, as the movement toward ethical franchising will likely shape the future of retail and service industries significantly.

Innovations in Customer Experience

Innovations in customer experience are reshaping the landscape of retail franchising, creating new opportunities for entrepreneurs and investors across various niches. As businesses strive to differentiate themselves in an increasingly competitive market, the integration of technology and personalized service has become paramount. The emergence of advanced customer relationship management tools, artificial intelligence, and data analytics enables franchises to tailor their offerings to meet the specific needs and preferences of their customers. This shift not only enhances customer satisfaction but also drives loyalty, a critical factor in the long-term success of any franchise.

In the food and beverage sector, innovations such as mobile ordering and contactless payment systems have transformed how customers interact with brands. Quick-service restaurants and cafes are leveraging these technologies to streamline operations and reduce wait times, creating a more efficient dining experience. Additionally, the use of augmented reality menus allows customers to visualize their food choices before ordering, enhancing their engagement and satisfaction. For entrepreneurs in this niche, investing in such technologies can lead to increased sales and a stronger competitive edge.

Health and fitness franchising has also seen significant advancements in customer experience through the incorporation of wearable technology and personalized fitness plans. Gyms and studios are now offering apps that track individual progress, provide tailored workout recommendations, and facilitate community engagement among members. This personalized approach not only fosters a sense of belonging but also encourages clients to remain committed to their fitness goals. For investors, franchises that prioritize technology integration and customer engagement in this sector are likely to see higher retention rates and increased revenue.

Retail franchising is experiencing a similar transformation, as businesses adopt omnichannel strategies to enhance the shopping experience. The integration of online and offline channels allows customers to interact with brands seamlessly, whether they are browsing in-store, shopping online, or using click-and-collect services. This strategy not only caters to the evolving preferences of consumers but also provides valuable data that can inform inventory management and marketing strategies. Entrepreneurs looking to enter the retail space should prioritize franchises that embrace these innovations to stay relevant and competitive.

Service-based franchising, including sectors like education and tutoring, is also leveraging technology to improve customer experiences. Online platforms are enabling personalized learning experiences, allowing tutors to tailor their methods to individual student needs. Moreover, the use of virtual reality in educational settings enhances engagement and retention, making learning more interactive and enjoyable. For investors, the focus on customer experience innovations in this niche presents opportunities for growth and expansion, as families increasingly seek convenient and effective educational solutions. By understanding and implementing these innovations, franchise owners can significantly enhance their value proposition and drive success in their respective markets.

Preparing for Disruptive Changes in the Market

Preparing for disruptive changes in the market is essential for entrepreneurs and investors in the franchising sector. Disruption can stem from various sources, including technological advancements, shifts in consumer preferences, economic fluctuations, and unforeseen global events like pandemics. Understanding these potential disruptions and proactively strategizing can position businesses to not only survive but thrive in a changing landscape. This preparation involves comprehensive market research, scenario planning, and building a resilient business model that can adapt to these changes.

Market research plays a pivotal role in anticipating disruptive changes. Entrepreneurs should continuously analyze industry trends, customer behavior, and competitor strategies to identify emerging threats and opportunities. This involves keeping an eye on innovations in technology, such as artificial intelligence and automation, which can significantly alter operational processes in sectors like retail and food and beverage franchising. By leveraging data analytics tools, franchisors can gain insights into consumer habits, enabling them to pivot their offerings and marketing strategies as needed. Staying informed and responsive can help businesses remain relevant in a fast-evolving marketplace.

Scenario planning is another critical aspect of preparing for disruption. Entrepreneurs should develop multiple scenarios that encompass various potential futures, considering factors such as economic downturns, changes in regulations, or shifts in consumer sentiment. This proactive approach allows businesses to establish contingency plans that can be activated when specific triggers occur. For instance, in the health and fitness franchising sector, preparing for a surge in demand for home-based workout solutions can help franchises transition swiftly in response to changing consumer needs. By envisioning different possibilities, businesses can foster an agile mindset that embraces change rather than fearing it.

Building a resilient business model is vital for navigating disruptions effectively. This involves diversifying revenue streams, enhancing operational flexibility, and investing in technology that facilitates adaptability. For instance, service-based franchises can explore digital service delivery options, allowing them to continue operations during unforeseen disruptions. Similarly, e-commerce franchising can benefit from robust online platforms that accommodate shifts in consumer shopping behavior. By incorporating flexibility into their models, franchises can respond quickly to market changes, ensuring continuity and growth even in challenging times.

Lastly, fostering a culture of innovation within the organization is essential for long-term success in the face of disruption. Encouraging employees to share ideas and experiment with new approaches can lead to creative solutions that address emerging challenges. Whether it's through investing in employee training or creating collaborative environments, businesses that prioritize innovation are better equipped to adapt to changes in their market. In a dynamic franchising landscape, having a workforce that is engaged and empowered to drive change can be a decisive advantage, allowing companies to navigate disruptive changes with confidence and agility.

www.ingramcontent.com/pod-product-compliance
Lightning Source LLC
Chambersburg PA
CBHW070205230526
45471CB00002B/824